Wonderful ways to prepare

MEATS

by ANNETTE HALCOMB

OTHER TITLES IN THIS SERIES

Printed in Canada.

Wonderful ways to prepare

MEATS

PLAYMORE INC NEW YORK USA
UNDER ARRANGEMENT WITH
I. WALDMAN & SON INC

AYERS & JAMES PTY LTD
CROWS NEST AUSTRALIA

STAFFORD PEMBERTON PUBLISHING
KNUTSFORD UNITED KINGDOM

FIRST PUBLISHED 1978

PUBLISHED IN THE USA
BY PLAYMORE INC.
UNDER ARRANGEMENT WITH I. WALDMAN & SON INC.

PUBLISHED IN AUSTRALIA
BY AYERS & JAMES PTY. LTD.
CROWS NEST.   AUSTRALIA

PUBLISHED IN THE UNITED KINGDOM
BY STAFFORD PEMBERTON PUBLISHING
KNUTSFORD CHESIRE

ISBN 0 86908 056 3

OVEN TEMPERATURE GUIDE

Description	Gas		Electric		Mark
	C	F	C	F	
Cool	100	200	110	225	¼
Very Slow	120	250	120	250	½
Slow	150	300	150	300	1-2
Moderately slow	160	325	170	340	3
Moderate	180	350	200	400	4
Moderately hot	190	375	220	425	5-6
Hot	200	400	230	450	6-7
Very hot	230	450	250	475	8-9

LIQUID MEASURES

IMPERIAL	METRIC
1 teaspoon	5 ml
1 tablespoon	20 ml
2 fluid ounces (¼ cup)	62.5 ml
4 fluid ounces (½ cup)	125 ml
8 fluid ounces (1 cup)	250 ml
1 pint (16 ounces — 2 cups)*	500 ml
* (The imperial pint is equal to 20 fluid ounces.)	

SOLID MEASURES

AVOIRDUPOIS	METRIC
1 ounce	30 g
4 ounces (¼ lb)	125 g
8 ounces (½ lb)	250 g
12 ounces (¾ lb)	375 g
16 ounces (1 lb)	500 g
24 ounces (1½ lb)	750 g
32 ounces (2 lb)	1000 g (1 kg)

CUP AND SPOON REPLACEMENTS FOR OUNCES

INGREDIENT	½ oz	1 oz	2 oz	3 oz	4 oz	5 oz	6 oz	7 oz	8 oz
Almonds, ground	2 T	¼ C	½ C	¾ C	1¼ C	1⅓ C	1⅔ C	2 C	2¼ C
slivered	6 t	¼ C	½ C	¾ C	1 C	1⅓ C	1⅔ C	2 C	2¼ C
whole	2 T	¼ C	⅓ C	½ C	¾ C	1 C	1¼ C	1⅓ C	1½ C
Apples, dried whole	3 T	½ C	1 C	1⅓ C	2 C	2⅓ C	2¾ C	3⅓ C	3¾ C
Apricots, chopped	2 T	¼ C	½ C	¾ C	1 C	1¼ C	1½ C	1¾ C	2 C
whole	2 T	3 T	½ C	⅔ C	1 C	1¼ C	1⅓ C	1½ C	1¾ C
Arrowroot	1 T	2 T	⅓ C	½ C	⅔ C	¾ C	1 C	1¼ C	1⅓ C
Baking Powder	1 T	2 T	⅓ C	½ C	⅔ C	¾ C	1 C	1 C	1¼ C
Baking Soda	1 T	2 T	⅓ C	½ C	⅔ C	¾ C	1 C	1 C	1¼ C
Barley	1 T	2 T	¼ C	½ C	⅔ C	¾ C	1 C	1 C	1¼ C
Breadcrumbs, dry	2 T	¼ C	½ C	¾ C	1 C	1¼ C	1½ C	1¾ C	2 C
soft	¼ C	½ C	1 C	1½ C	2 C	2½ C	3 C	3⅔ C	4¼ C
Biscuit Crumbs	2 T	¼ C	½ C	¾ C	1¼ C	1⅓ C	1⅔ C	2 C	2¼ C
Butter	3 t	6 t	¼ C	⅓ C	½ C	⅔ C	¾ C	1 C	1 C
Cheese, grated, lightly packed,									
natural cheddar	6 t	¼ C	½ C	¾ C	1 C	1¼ C	1½ C	1¾ C	2 C
Processed cheddar	5 t	2 T	⅓ C	⅔ C	¾ C	1 C	1¼ C	1½ C	1⅔ C
Parmesan, Romano	6 t	¼ C	½ C	¾ C	1 C	1⅓ C	1⅔ C	2 C	2¼ C
Cherries, candied, chopped	1 T	2 T	⅓ C	½ C	¾ C	1 C	1 C	1⅓ C	1½ C
whole	1 T	2 T	⅓ C	½ C	⅔ C	¾ C	1 C	1¼ C	1⅓ C
Cocoa	2 T	¼ C	½ C	¾ C	1¼ C	1⅓ C	1⅔ C	2 C	2¼ C
Coconut, desiccated	2 T	⅓ C	⅔ C	1 C	1⅓ C	1⅔ C	2 C	2⅓ C	2⅔ C
shredded	⅓ C	⅔ C	1¼ C	1¾ C	2½ C	3 C	3⅔ C	4⅓ C	5 C
Cornstarch	6 t	3 T	½ C	⅔ C	1 C	1¼ C	1½ C	1⅔ C	2 C
Corn Syrup	2 t	1 T	2 T	¼ C	⅓ C	½ C	½ C	⅔ C	⅔ C
Coffee, ground	2 T	⅓ C	⅔ C	1 C	1⅓ C	1⅔ C	2 C	2⅓ C	2⅔ C
instant	3 T	½ C	1 C	1⅓ C	1¾ C	2¼ C	2⅔ C	3 C	3½ C
Cornflakes	½ C	1 C	2 C	3 C	4¼ C	5¼ C	6¼ C	7⅓ C	8⅓ C
Cream of Tartar	1 T	2 T	⅓ C	½ C	⅔ C	¾ C	1 C	1 C	1¼ C
Currants	1 T	2 T	⅓ C	⅔ C	¾ C	1 C	1¼ C	1½ C	1⅔ C
Custard Powder	6 t	3 T	½ C	⅔ C	1 C	1¼ C	1½ C	1⅔ C	2 C
Dates, chopped	1 T	2 T	⅓ C	⅔ C	¾ C	1 C	1¼ C	1½ C	1⅔ C
whole, pitted	1 T	2 T	⅓ C	½ C	¾ C	1 C	1¼ C	1⅓ C	1½ C
Figs, chopped	1 T	2 T	⅓ C	½ C	¾ C	1 C	1 C	1⅓ C	1½ C
Flour, all-purpose or cake	6 t	¼ C	½ C	¾ C	1 C	1¼ C	1½ C	1¾ C	2 C
wholemeal	6 t	3 T	½ C	⅔ C	1 C	1¼ C	1⅓ C	1⅔ C	1¾ C
Fruit, mixed	1 T	2 T	⅓ C	½ C	¾ C	1 C	1¼ C	1⅓ C	1½ C
Gelatine	5 t	2 T	⅓ C	½ C	¾ C	1 C	1 C	1¼ C	1½ C
Ginger, crystallised pieces	1 T	2 T	⅓ C	½ C	¾ C	1 C	1¼ C	1⅓ C	1½ C
ground	6 t	⅓ C	½ C	¾ C	1¼ C	1½ C	1¾ C	2 C	2¼ C
preserved, heavy syrup	1 T	2 T	⅓ C	½ C	⅔ C	¾ C	1 C	1 C	1¼ C
Glucose, liquid	2 t	1 T	2 T	¼ C	⅓ C	½ C	½ C	⅔ C	⅔ C
Haricot Beans	1 T	2 T	⅓ C	½ C	⅔ C	¾ C	1 C	1 C	1¼ C

In this table, t represents teaspoonful, T represents tablespoonful and C represents cupful.

CUP AND SPOON REPLACEMENTS FOR OUNCES (Cont.)

INGREDIENT	½ oz	1 oz	2 oz	3 oz	4 oz	5 oz	6 oz	7 oz	8 oz
Honey	2 t	1 T	2 T	¼ C	⅓ C	½ C	½ C	⅔ C	⅔ C
Jam	2 t	1 T	2 T	¼ C	⅓ C	½ C	½ C	⅔ C	¾ C
Lentils	1 T	2 T	⅓ C	½ C	⅔ C	¾ C	1 C	1 C	1¼ C
Macaroni (see pasta)									
Milk Powder, full cream	2 T	¼ C	½ C	¾ C	1¼ C	1⅓ C	1⅔ C	2 C	2¼ C
non fat	2 T	⅓ C	¾ C	1¼ C	1½ C	2 C	2⅓ C	2¾ C	3¼ C
Nutmeg	6 t	3 T	½ C	⅔ C	¾ C	1 C	1¼ C	1½ C	1⅔ C
Nuts, chopped	6 t	¼ C	½ C	¾ C	1 C	1¼ C	1½ C	1¾ C	2 C
Oatmeal	1 T	2 T	½ C	⅔ C	¾ C	1 C	1¼ C	1½ C	1⅔ C
Olives, whole	1 T	2 T	⅓ C	⅔ C	¾ C	1 C	1¼ C	1½ C	1⅔ C
sliced	1 T	2 T	⅓ C	⅔ C	¾ C	1 C	1¼ C	1½ C	1⅔ C
Pasta, short (e.g. macaroni)	1 T	2 T	⅓ C	⅔ C	¾ C	1 C	1¼ C	1½ C	1⅔ C
Peaches, dried & whole	1 T	2 T	⅓ C	⅔ C	¾ C	1 C	1¼ C	1½ C	1⅔ C
chopped	6 t	¼ C	½ C	¾ C	1 C	1¼ C	1½ C	1¾ C	2 C
Peanuts, shelled, raw, whole	1 T	2 T	⅓ C	½ C	¾ C	1 C	1¼ C	1⅓ C	1½ C
roasted	1 T	2 T	⅓ C	⅔ C	¾ C	1 C	1¼ C	1½ C	1⅔ C
Peanut Butter	3 t	6 t	3 T	⅓ C	½ C	½ C	⅔ C	¾ C	1 C
Peas, split	1 T	2 T	⅓ C	½ C	⅔ C	¾ C	1 C	1 C	1¼ C
Peel, mixed	1 T	2 T	⅓ C	½ C	¾ C	1 C	1 C	1¼ C	1½ C
Potato, powder	1 T	2 T	¼ C	⅓ C	½ C	⅔ C	¾ C	1 C	1¼ C
flakes	¼ C	½ C	1 C	1⅓ C	2 C	2⅓ C	2¾ C	3⅓ C	3¾ C
Prunes, chopped	1 T	2 T	⅓ C	½ C	⅔ C	¾ C	1 C	1¼ C	1⅓ C
whole pitted	1 T	2 T	⅓ C	½ C	⅔ C	¾ C	1 C	1 C	1¼ C
Raisins	2 T	¼ C	⅓ C	½ C	¾ C	1 C	1 C	1⅓ C	1½ C
Rice, short grain, raw	1 T	2 T	¼ C	½ C	⅔ C	¾ C	1 C	1 C	1¼ C
long grain, raw	1 T	2 T	⅓ C	½ C	¾ C	1 C	1¼ C	1⅓ C	1½ C
Rice Bubbles	⅔ C	1¼ C	2½ C	3⅔ C	5 C	6¼ C	7½ C	8¾ C	10 C
Rolled Oats	2 T	⅓ C	⅔ C	1 C	1⅓ C	1¾ C	2 C	2½ C	2¾ C
Sago	2 T	¼ C	⅓ C	½ C	¾ C	1 C	1 C	1¼ C	1½ C
Salt, common	3 t	6 t	¼ C	⅓ C	½ C	⅔ C	¾ C	1 C	1 C
Semolina	1 T	2 T	⅓ C	½ C	¾ C	1 C	1 C	1⅓ C	1½ C
Spices	6 t	3 T	¼ C	⅓ C	½ C	½ C	⅔ C	¾ C	1 C
Sugar, plain	3 t	6 t	¼ C	⅓ C	½ C	⅔ C	¾ C	1 C	1 C
confectioners'	1 T	2 T	⅓ C	½ C	¾ C	1 C	1 C	1¼ C	1½ C
moist brown	1 T	2 T	⅓ C	½ C	¾ C	1 C	1 C	1⅓ C	1½ C
Tapioca	1 T	2 T	⅓ C	½ C	⅔ C	¾ C	1 C	1¼ C	1⅓ C
Treacle	2 t	1 T	2 T	¼ C	⅓ C	½ C	½ C	⅔ C	⅔ C
Walnuts, chopped	2 T	¼ C	½ C	¾ C	1 C	1¼ C	1½ C	1¾ C	2 C
halved	2 T	⅓ C	⅔ C	1 C	1¼ C	1½ C	1¾ C	2¼ C	2½ C
Yeast, dried	6 t	3 T	½ C	⅔ C	1 C	1¼ C	1⅓ C	1⅔ C	1¾ C
compressed	3 t	6 t	3 T	⅓ C	½ C	½ C	⅔ C	¾ C	1 C

In this table, t represents teaspoonful, T represents tablespoonful and C represents cupful.

Contents

Choosing Your Meat

Beef Hindquarter Retail Cuts and Cooking Uses

1. SHORT LOIN

In One Piece: Roasting
Steaks (Porterhouse, T-Bone, Club): Broiling, frying, barbecuing
Tenderloin or fillet: Roasting, frying

2. SIRLOIN

Steaks (Sirloin, Pin Bone Sirloin): Broiling, frying, barbecuing
In One Piece: Roasting

3. FLANK

Boned and Rolled: Roasting
Chopped: Braising, stewing
Steak: Broiling, frying

4. RUMP

In One Piece: Roasting
Rolled: Roasting

Steaks: Grilling, frying, barbecuing

5. ROUND

In One Piece: Roasting, pot roasting
Steaks: Frying, braising
Ground: Meat loaf, hamburgers, meat sauces

6. HEEL OF ROUND

Whole: Stewing
Corned: Simmering, glazing

7. HIND SHANK

Whole: Roasting, pot roasting.
Steaks: Broiling, frying, braising

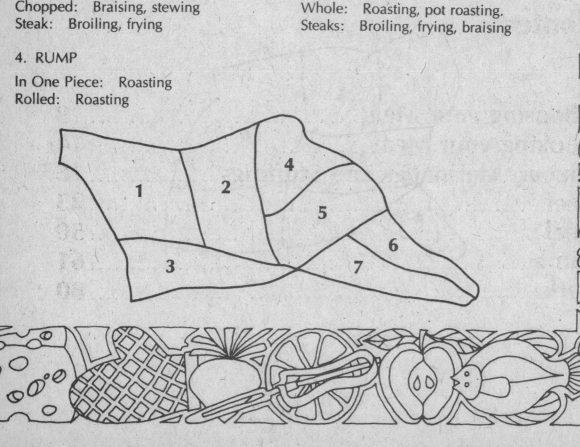

9

Beef Forequarter Retail Cuts and Cooking Uses

1. NECK

Boned and Rolled: Roasting

2. SHOULDER

Boned and Rolled: Roasting
English cut

3. BRISKET

Boned and Rolled: Pot roasting
Corned: Simmering

4. FORESHANK

Pieces: Soup stock, brawn
Boned: Soup stock, stewing,
casseroling

5. CHUCK

Boned and Rolled: Pot roast
Steaks: Stewing, braising

6. RIB

Boned and Rolled: Roasting
Short Ribs: Braising, stewing,
barbecuing
One Piece with Bone: Roasting
Steaks: Broiling, frying,
barbecuing

7. SHORT PLATE

Boned and Rolled: Roasting
Cut into Steaks: Broiling, frying

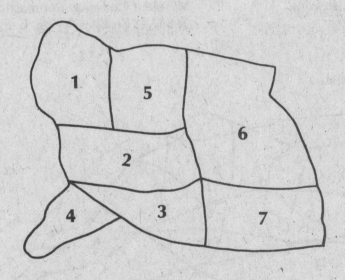

Veal
Retail Cuts and Cooking Uses

1. NECK

Chopped: Stewing

2. SHOULDER

Boned and Rolled: Roasting
Chopped: Braising, stewing, casseroling

3. FORESHANK

Chopped: Stewing

4. RIB

Chops: Broiling
Crown roast
Rib roast

5. BREAST

In One Piece: Roasting
Chopped: Braising, stewing, casseroling
Boned and Rolled: Roasting
Ground: Meat loaves, meat balls, stuffings

6. LOIN

Cutlets: Broiling, frying, braising
Chops: Broiling, frying, braising
Sirloin Steak

7. FLANK

Ground: Meat loaf

8. RUMP

In One Piece with Bone: Roasting
Boned and Rolled: Roasting

9. LEG

Scallops or cutlets: Broiling, frying
One Piece with Bone: Roast

10. HEEL OF ROUND: Roast

11. HIND SHANK

With Bone: Soup stock, stewing

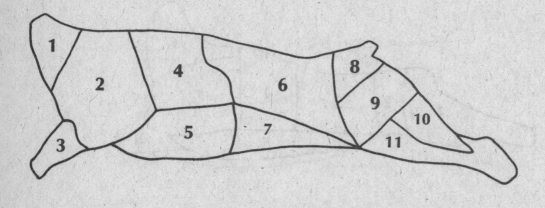

Lamb
Retail Cuts and Cooking Uses

1. LEG

In One Piece: Roasting
Boned and Rolled: Roasting, braising
Chops: Frying, broiling, braising

2. SIRLOIN LAMB ROAST

In One Piece: Roasting

3. LOIN

In One Piece: Roasting
Chops: Broiling, frying, barbecuing
Boned and Rolled: Roasting

4. RACK

Lamb Crown Roast: Roasting
Chops: Broiling, frying

5. BREAST

Boned and Rolled: Braising, roasting
In One Piece: Baking
Lamb Riblets: Stewing

6. NECK

Lamb Neck Slices: Braising, frying, broiling

7. SHOULDER

In One Piece: Roasting
Boned and Rolled: Roasting
Chops: Frying, broiling, braising, barbecuing

8. SHANK: Braising, stewing.

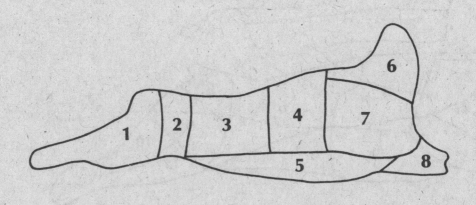

Pork
Retail Cuts and Cooking
Uses

1. SHOULDER BUTT

In One Piece: Roasting
Chops: Broiling, frying, braising,
barbecuing

2. SHOULDER (PICNIC)

In One Piece: Roasting
Smoked: Ham

3. HOCK

Cut Up: Stewing, braising

4. FOREFOOT

5. FAT BACK

Lard, salt pork, shortening

6. LOIN

Whole: Roasting
Sliced: Canadian bacon, frying
Chops: Broiling, frying,
barbecuing

7. SPARERIBS

In One Piece or
Separated: Broiling, baking,
barbecuing

8. FLANK

Sliced Bacon: Frying

9. HAM

In One Piece with
Bone: Roasting
Boned and Rolled: Roasting
Sliced: Broiling, barbecuing

10. HIND FOOT

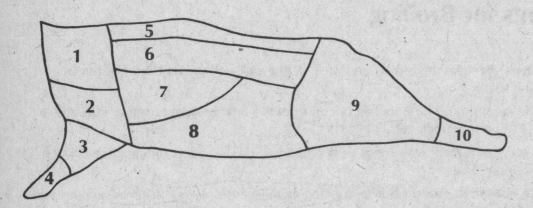

Cooking Your Meat

Hints for Roasting

1. Always have your baking dish large enough. Make sure the meat does not extend over the sides.

2. A rack in the baking dish helps good circulation of heat around the meat and should be used if meat has no bone.

3. The meat should be at room temperature before cooking. Rub the meat with salt on the fat side only as the salt draws out the juices from the meat. Pepper may be added to the meat part only.

4. Meat cooked in a moderate oven is tastier and more tender than meat cooked at high temperatures. Fillet of beef is an exception to this rule as well as pork with rind (to crisp the rind).

5. If you are using a meat thermometer it is wise to use it at the end of the cooking time. It should be inserted with the tip in the center of the thickest part of the meat and it should not touch the bone. Never use your thermometer in high oven temperatures.

6. Always rest the meat for at least 15 minutes before carving. This makes the meat easier to carve, more tender and seals in the juices.

Hints for Broiling

1. Always preheat the broiler and rack. A hot rack will prevent the meat from sticking to it.

2. The meat should be 2 inches (5 cm) from the heat or flame for thin cuts and 3 inches (8 cm) for thick cuts.

3. Always turn meat with tongs or two spoons. This prevents piercing the surface and loosing juices.

4. Do not salt the meat prior to cooking as this causes a loss of juices. Pepper may be added to taste.

5. Broil the meat for approximately 2 minutes on the first side, turn and repeat the process turning every 2 minutes until the meat is done.

Hints for Frying

1. The butter or oil should just cover the bottom of the frying pan for ordinary meats. If breaded meats are used, the oil or butter must come halfway up the sides of the meat.

2. The meat should be only turned once during cooking. When turning use tongs or two spoons so as not to pierce the meat. When turning breaded meat use spatula so as not to break the coating.

3. If breaded meats are to be kept warm, never cover as this will soften the coating.

Hints for Casseroling and Stewing

1. Do not overcrowd the pan when browning the meat. Brown a little at a time. Always make sure the pan is large enough to hold the meat and vegetables for the balance of the cooking.

2. Always bring the meat to a slow simmer, cover and cook gently until the meat is tender. Never boil or the meat will become tough.

3. If there is time, it is a good method to stop and seal the cooking halfway through. Leave the meat to sit for about 1 hour, before continuing the cooking. The meat takes in all the flavors.

Roasting Timetable

MEAT	TIME	OVEN TEMP.		MEAT THERMOMETER		
		C	F	C	F	
Beef	30 minutes per lb (60 minutes per kg) for medium beef. If rare or well done beef is required, adjust the time.	180	350	60 70 75	140 160 170	Rare Medium Well done
Lamb	30 minutes per lb (60 minutes per kg)	180	350	75 80	170 180	Medium Well done
Pork	45 minutes per lb (90 minutes per kg)	180	350	85	185	Well done
Veal	45 minutes per lb (90 minutes per kg)	180	350	75	170	Well done

Sauces, Marinades and Stuffings

Bearnaise Sauce

¾ cup (187.5 ml) dry white wine
¼ cup (63 ml) tarragon vinegar
1 tablespoon chopped parsley
1 tablespoon chopped scallions
½ teaspoon dried tarragon
freshly ground black pepper

1 teaspoon cornstarch
3 egg yolks
1 tablespoon boiling water
½ cup (125 g) butter
salt

1. Put the wine, vinegar, scallions, parsley, tarragon and pepper in a saucepan and bring the mixture to the boil. Cook until the liquid is reduced to half the original amount.
2. Add a little wine to the cornstarch in a cup and mix until smooth. Add to the reduced liquid and thicken. Cool for 1 minute.
3. Pour into the top section of a double boiler and place over simmering, not boiling water. Mix well.
4. Mix the egg yolks with 1 tablespoon of boiling water and add this to the wine mixture stirring constantly.
5. Add the butter, 1 tablespoon at a time making sure each lot is completely absorbed before adding the next tablespoon. Add salt and pepper to taste before serving. This sauce may be kept warm over hot water. Be careful not to curdle.

Mushroom Sauce

8 oz (250 g) button mushrooms
1 cup (250 ml) white wine
2 tablespoons (40 g) butter
juice of 1 lemon
2 tablespoons flour

2 tablespoons brandy
½ cup cream
salt and white pepper
1 tablespoon of fresh or
   dried chives

1. Trim the mushrooms and place the trimmings in a saucepan with ½ cup of the wine and simmer, covered for 15 minutes. Strain and reserve the liquid.
2. Slice the mushrooms and sauté in a pan with 1 tablespoon of the butter and add the lemon juice. Take the mushrooms out of the pan and put aside.
3. Melt the remaining butter in the pan, stir in the flour until smooth and cook for 1 minute. Add the reserved mushroom liquid, wine, brandy and cook stirring constantly, until the sauce is smooth and thick. Add the mushrooms and cook for a further 2 minutes.
4. Stir in the cream and season to taste. Add the chives and heat again without boiling.

Mint Sauce

mint leaves
8 oz (250 g) sugar
16 oz (500 ml) vinegar

1. Using very fresh mint chop finely and half fill sterilized jars.
2. Heat the vinegar in a saucepan and stir in the sugar until dissolved and bring to the boil. Cool.
3. Fill the jars containing mint with the vinegar and sugar mixture. Seal immediately. Let stand for at least one day. If the mixture is too sour it can be diluted by adding hot water to taste.

Quick Mint Sauce

8 teaspoons dried mint
4 tablespoons sugar

1 oz (30 ml) water
6 tablespoons vinegar

Bring the water to boil in a saucepan and add the dried mint, then the sugar until dissolved. Remove from the heat and add the vinegar. If too strong or too weak add less or more vinegar.

Tomato and Wine Sauce

2 onions, chopped
3 cloves garlic, crushed
3 tablespoons oil
½ cup tomato paste
2 cups, chopped peeled tomatoes
1 bay leaf, crushed

2 tablespoons chopped parsley
1 teaspoon basil
1 cup (250 ml) red or dry white wine
1 teaspoon brown sugar
salt and freshly ground black
   pepper

1. Sauté the onion and garlic in oil until soft but not brown.
2. Stir in all the other ingredients. Season to taste.
3. Cover and cook for 1 hour stirring occasionally.

Serve with meat balls, meat loaf, hamburgers, beef fondues and spaghetti dishes.

Fruity Marinade

1 cup pineapple or orange juice
1 teaspoon curry powder
½ cup honey
2 cloves garlic

½ teaspoon nutmeg
freshly ground black pepper
¼ cup salad oil

Mix all the ingredients together and pour over the meat.

This marinade is used for lamb and pork.

Plum Sauce

1 can (425 g) plums
2 small onions, chopped
1 clove garlic, crushed
1 tablespoon oil
½ teaspoon allspice
½ teaspoon ground ginger

pinch ground cloves
pinch hot chilli pepper
salt and pepper
1 tablespoon brown sugar
2 tablespoons malt or cider vinegar

1. Press plums and liquid through a sieve or remove stones and blend in a blender.
2. Sauté the onion and garlic in the oil until soft but not brown. Add the plums and the rest of the ingredients. Cover and cook slowly for 20 minutes. Thicken with cornflour if desired.

This sauce is delicious served with roast pork, most barbecued meats, beef fondue, and served cold with cold meats and corned meats.

Wine Marinade

1 cup (250 ml) red or white wine
½ cup salad oil
2 sliced onions
1 sliced lemon
2 cloves garlic
1 bay leaf

6 whole black peppercorns
mixed herbs e.g. tarragon, basil
  or thyme for beef
rosemary, mint, thyme or oregano
  for lamb

Mix all the ingredients together and add the appropriate herbs.

Hawaiian Marinade

½ cup (125 ml) pineapple or orange
  juice
½ cup (125 ml) oil
¼ cup (63 ml) soya sauce
2 tablespoons lemon juice

1 teaspoon dry mustard
1 tablespoon honey
½ teaspoon ground ginger
½ teaspoon mace
½ cup brown sugar

Mix all the ingredients together.

This marinade is used for beef and pork cuts. Ideal for barbecuing, especially lamb shanks.

Maitre d'Hotel Butter

½ cup (125 g) butter
salt and pepper
3 tablespoons chopped parsley
2 tablespoons lemon juice

Soften the butter and blend in all the ingredients. Place in a small butter crock and cover and chill.

The butter can also be shaped into a roll and wrapped. When chilled slice into rounds.

Serve with beef, lamb and veal.

Lemon Herb Stuffing

grated rind and juice of
  2 lemons
1½ cups soft breadcrumbs
1 teaspoon thyme

½ teaspoon marjoram
salt and pepper
½ teaspoon sage
1 beaten egg

Mix all the dry ingredients together, add the juice of the lemons and bind with the beaten egg.

This is used for lamb, beef olives and veal birds.

Bacon and Herb Stuffing

3 slices bacon
1 tablespoon (20 g) butter
2 small onions, finely chopped
1½ cups soft breadcrumbs
2 tablespoons chopped parsley

½ teaspoon thyme
½ teaspoon basil
salt and pepper
1 egg, beaten

1. Cook bacon until just crisp. Add the butter and onion and cook until the onion is soft but not brown.
2. Mix into breadcrumbs with the herbs and add salt and pepper to taste and add the beaten egg and mix well.

This is a fine stuffing for lamb, veal and beef.

Fruity Rice Stuffing

2 small onions, grated
2 tablespoons (40 g) butter
1 cup cooked rice
1 tablespoon chopped raisins
1 tablespoon chopped dried
   apricots

1 tablespoon dried currants
1 tablespoon pine nuts
1 tablespoon grated lemon rind
juice of 1 lemon
salt and pepper
1 beaten egg

1. Sauté onion in the butter until soft but not brown. Stir in the rice, raisins, currants and apricots and cook for 4 minutes.
2. Remove from the heat and cool. Stir in pine nuts, lemon rind and juice and salt and pepper to taste. Bind with the beaten egg.

This is used for veal, lamb or pork.

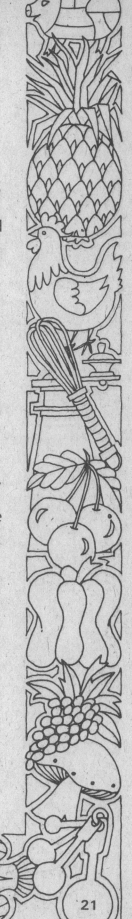

Orange Stuffing

2 tablespoons (40 g) butter
1 medium onion, chopped
2 cups soft breadcrumbs
1 egg, beaten
1 tablespoon chopped parsley

grated rind and juice of 2
  oranges
salt and pepper to taste
1 tablespoon Grand Marnier
  or Cointreau (optional)

1. Sauté the onions in butter until soft but not brown.
2. Add the onions to breadcrumbs with all the other ingredients. Bind well and add the Grand Marnier or Cointreau if desired.

This is nice used in lamb and pork.

Mint Jelly

2 lb (1 kg) green apples
5 cups (1200 ml) water
juice of 2 lemons

bunch of fresh mint
sugar
green coloring

1. Slice the apples but do not remove the cores. Place in a saucepan with the water, lemon juice and several sprigs of mint (about 10). Bring to the boil and cook slowly until the mixture is a soft pulp, break the apples up.
2. Strain the liquid through a piece of muslin, a piece of fine linen or a very fine sieve into a bowl. Allow to drip overnight. Do not squeeze the muslin to hasten dripping as the jelly will then be cloudy.
3. Measure the juice that has been strained, place in a saucepan and bring to the boil. Add 1½ cups (375 g) sugar for every cup (250 ml) of strained juice, stir again and bring to boil.
4. If the flavor of the mixture is not strong enough a little fresh mint may be added. Continue boiling removing the scum when necessary and boil until the mixture sets. Test the mixture for setting by spooning a little onto a cold saucer. It is ready when a skin forms on the surface which will wrinkle when you run your finger over the surface.
5. Add a little green coloring and pour into heated and sterilized jars and cover immediately.

Beef

Pepper Steak

4 portions fillet steak	½ teaspoon Worcestershire sauce
2 tablespoons black peppercorns	1 tablespoon lemon juice
1 tablespoon (20 g) butter	2 tablespoons brandy
salt	2 tablespoons cream

1. Crack the peppercorns by placing them in a plastic or paper bag and hitting them with a mallet, or using a mortar and pestle. Coat the steak with the cracked pepper, pressing it well into the steak with the heel of the hand.
2. Heat the butter in a frying pan and add the steaks. Cook over a high heat, 1 minute each side to seal the juices. Cook over a moderate heat until cooked to your taste (6 minutes for a medium done steak). Sprinkle over Worcestershire sauce and lemon juice and warm the brandy, light and pour over the steaks. When flames have died down, lift the steaks onto a plate and season with salt.
3. Pour the cream into pan juices and mix quickly. Pour over the steaks and serve immediately.

Serves 4.

Fillet Steak with Mushrooms

fillet steak
4 tablespoons (80 g) butter
1 teaspoon rosemary
salt and pepper

1 tablespoon Worcestershire sauce
1 teaspoon mustard
2 tablespoons brandy
1 cup sliced mushrooms

1. Slice the steak into wafer thin slices and fry in the butter and rosemary about 3 minutes each side.
2. Remove steak from the pan and keep warm. Add all the other ingredients to the pan and bring to the boil.
3. Pour over the steak and serve immediately.

This steak is nice served with rice and a green salad.

Serves 4-6.

Filet Mignon

6 slices fillet steak (1½ inches thick)
6 slices of bacon
freshly ground black pepper
4 tablespoons (80 g) butter
salt

1. Wrap a bacon slice around each fillet and fasten with a toothpick. Let stand at room temperature for 30 minutes.
2. Sprinkle each side with ground black pepper and place on a broiler rack.
3. Spread each fillet with a little butter and cook under a pre-heated broiler for 6 to 8 minutes, spreading the remainder of the butter on the fillet when turned. Do not pierce the steak when turning. Season with a little salt and serve.

The fillet is nice served with sautéed mushrooms or mushroom sauce.

Serves 6.

Fillet Steak Cynthia

1 fillet weighing about
    4 lb (2 kg)
2 grated carrots
rind of 1 lemon, grated
rind of 1 orange, grated
1 large onion, grated

2 tablespoons parsley, chopped
butter
cream
brandy
salt and freshly ground pepper

1. Place the fillet on a baking dish and rub with about 1 tablespoon butter, sprinkle with salt and freshly ground pepper.
2. Mix the carrots, rinds, onion and parsley together and cover the top of the fillet with the mixture. Cover with foil or plastic wrap and let stand at room temperature for at least 4 hours.
3. Bake in a hot oven 425°F (220°C) for 1 hour or until done to your taste.
4. Remove the fillet and keep warm. Add about 1 cup of cream and 2 tablespoons brandy to the drippings in the baking dish, thicken if desired and serve over the meat.

Serves 4.

Beef Cordon Bleu

6 oz (185 g) fillet cut to
    1 inch (2 cm) thickness
3 oz (90 g) butter
2 oz (63 ml) brandy
2 oz (60 g) mushrooms, sauteed

1 oz (30 ml) Bearnaise Sauce (see
    recipe)
1 slice ham
1 slice Swiss cheese

1. Sauté the fillet in butter to the right degree. Pour over the warmed brandy and flame.
2. Top the steaks with mushrooms and Bearnaise Sauce. Add the ham then broil for about 2 minutes. Add the cheese and broil until the cheese is melted.

Serves 1.

Fillet Steak with Scallion Butter

fillet steak	scallions
peanut oil	butter
garlic, crushed	salt and pepper
pepper, salt	

1. Mix peanut oil, garlic and salt and pepper together and marinate the steaks in this marinade for at least 3 hours at room temperature. Turn about every ½ hour.
2. Broil under a very hot flame for about 7 minutes or until done. Season.
3. Meanwhile mince a scallion finely and mix into about 1 tablespoon (20 g) butter and add salt and pepper.
4. When steak is cooked serve with a pat of the butter and scallions on top of the hot steak.

Brandied Fillet of Beef

2 lb (1 kg) fillet of beef	soya sauce
1 tablespoon olive oil	salt and freshly ground
2 tablespoons brandy	black pepper
1 clove garlic, crushed	butter mixed with 2 cloves of
1 tablespoon parsley	garlic, crushed
2 tablespoons lemon juice	

1. Mix oil, brandy, garlic, parsley, lemon juice, a dash of soya sauce, salt and pepper and place the beef in the mixture and marinate at room temperature for about 8 hours.
2. Place the fillets in foil and spread the garlic butter on the top of each fillet, sprinkle with a little parsley. Wrap in the foil sealing the edges and cook for about 1 hour in a moderate oven 350°F (180°C).

Serves 4.

Baked Fillet Steak

fillet steak
small piece of butter
1 tablespoon brown sugar
salt and pepper
pineapple

onion, chopped
2 tablespoons tomato sauce
1 tablespoon lemon juice
1 teaspoon soya sauce
parsley

1. Melt the butter and brown sugar and brown the steak in the mixture.
2. Place the browned meat in a baking dish and top each piece with a ring of pineapple and a little chopped onion. Pour a mixture of tomato sauce, lemon juice and soya sauce over the meat and season to taste.
3. Cover with buttered paper and cook very slowly for 45 minutes.
4. Remove the paper, top with pineapple and chopped parsley and serve.

Serves 4-6.

Swiss Steak

2 lb (1 kg) rump steak
sheet of aluminum foil
1 cup Plum Sauce (see recipe)
   or tomato sauce
½ cup flour
1 large onion, sliced

1. Mix the sauce with the flour and spoon half of the mixture on the foil in the middle. Put the steak on top of the sauce and top with sliced onion and remaining sauce. Fold and seal.
2. Bake in a hot oven 400°F (200°C) for 1½ hours.

Serves 4.

27

Sesame Beef Kebabs

1 lb (500 g) round or
  blade steak, thickly cut
1 tablespoon lemon juice
1 tablespoon oil
1 tablespoon grated onion
1 tablespoon grated peel
  from 1 lemon

¼ cup soya sauce
1 tablespoon brown sugar
1 garlic clove, crushed
½ teaspoon ginger
1 tablespoon sesame seeds

1. Cut the meat into 1 inch (2½ cm) cubes and marinate in a mixture of the rest of the ingredients for at least 3 hours at room temperature. Stir two or three times.
2. Remove the meat from the marinade and roll in some dry sesame seeds, thread onto a skewer and broil for 8-15 minutes.

Serves 4.

Royal Broil

2 flanks of skirt steak
4 tablespoons lemon juice
½ cup (125 ml) olive oil
ground black pepper
salt

1. Score the steak in a criss cross pattern on each side. Put in a flat dish and pour the lemon juice and oil over the steak. Add the pepper and allow to stand for 6 hours turning regularly. If the weather is hot place in the refrigerator.
2. Preheat the broiler and broil the steaks 10 minutes each side brushing regularly with the oil and lemon juice.
3. Lift onto a warm plate and allow to stand 5 minutes before carving. Carve downwards across the grain with a knife held at an angle of 45°. This method gives juicy slices.

Serves 4.

Carpet Bag Steak

1 slice middle-cut rump steak,
   cut 1½ inches (4 cm) thick
freshly ground black pepper
about 20 small oysters

1 tablespoon lemon juice
1 tablespoon (20 g) butter
salt
1 teaspoon cornstarch

1. Make a deep pocket in the steak. Rub the pocket with salt and black pepper. Pour the lemon juice over drained oysters. Reserve the oyster liquor together with a few oysters.
2. Fill the pocket with the oysters and close the pocket with toothpicks. Spread each fillet with half the butter.
3. Rub the steak with freshly ground black pepper.
4. Preheat the broiler and cook for 6 minutes each side spreading the balance of the butter on the other side of the steak.
5. Meanwhile reduce the oyster liquor in a saucepan to ½ cup. Add the reserved oysters, lemon juice and salt and pepper to taste. Mix the cornstarch in a little cold water and thicken the sauce. Cook for 1 minute.
6. Cut the steak into 1 inch (2½ cm) thick slices with a knife held at an angle, cut across grain of the meat.

Serves 4.

Stifado

1½ lb (750 g) round or blade
   steak, 1 inch (2½ cm) cubes
2 medium onions, finely chopped
3 cloves garlic, crushed
4 tablespoons olive oil
1½ cups (375 ml) tomato purée
1 cup (250 ml) red wine

1 bay leaf
small piece cinnamon stick
salt and freshly ground black pepper
2 teaspoons brown sugar
1 lb (500 g) small white onions
1 tablespoon currants

1. Brown the cubes of beef in oil until brown and transfer to a casserole dish. Sauté the onion and garlic in the pan until they are soft, add tomato purée, wine, bay leaf, cinnamon stick, salt and pepper, and brown sugar. Bring to the boil and pour over the meat in the casserole.
2. Cook in a moderate oven for 45 minutes. Add the prepared onions and sprinkle the currants on top. Cover and cook for a further 1½ hours or until the meat and onions are tender.

Cut a small cross at the root end of each skinned onion to prevent them from coming apart during the cooking process.

Serves 4-6.

Steak with Prunes

4 tablespoons brown sugar
2 lb (1 kg) rump steak
3 tablespoons flour
salt and pepper
½ teaspoon each of ground ginger,
   mustard, curry powder and
   mixed spices
3 tablespoons vinegar

3 tablespoons port wine
1 teaspoon Worcestershire sauce
2 tablespoons tomato sauce
grated rind and juice of 1 lemon
2 slices bacon, finely chopped
½ lb (250 g) chopped prunes
1 tablespoon chopped parsley
3 sliced onions

1. Heat the sugar in a heavy saucepan until well browned.
2. Cut the steak into 1 inch (2½ cm) cubes, roll in flour and salt and pepper and brown in the sugar.
3. Add the sliced onions and cook until all the meat and onion are well covered with caramel.
4. Mix in all the other ingredients and cook very slowly for at least 2 hours.

Serves 4-6.

Steak Argentine

4 lb (2 kg) blade steak
2 tablespoons brown sugar
2 tablespoons flour
1 teaspoon curry powder
1 teaspoon ground ginger
1 cup (250 ml) port

½ cup (125 ml) vinegar
juice of lemon
grated lemon rind
grated cheese
chopped bacon
prunes, seeded

1. Cut steak into 2 inch (5 cm) cubes and place on a flat dish. Cover the meat with sugar, flour, curry powder and ground ginger. Pour over the port, tomato sauce, vinegar, lemon juice, lemon rind, grated cheese and bacon. Marinate for several hours.
2. Bake covered with tinfoil for 2 hours. After the first hour of baking add a handful of prunes.

This dish should be prepared the night before or early the same morning so that the juices soak through the meat.

Serves 6.

Roast Beef with Oyster Stuffing

4 lb (2 kg) beef round
salt
freshly ground black pepper
2 small onions, grated
2 tablespoons (40 g) butter

10 oysters, bottled or fresh
juice of 1 lemon
½ cup soft breadcrumbs
1 tablespoon chopped parsley

1. Cut a pocket into the corner of the beef round.
2. Cook the onions in a little butter until soft. Mix with the oysters, lemon juice, breadcrumbs and parsley. Season to taste.
3. Fill the pocket with the stuffing and secure with skewers.
4. Face the fat-side up on a rack in a roasting pan and rub the meat over with salt and pepper, top and bottom.
5. Roast in a moderate oven 350°F (180°C) for 30 minutes per pound (1 hour per kg).
6. Make a gravy by adding a little flour and some water or beef stock to the drippings.

Serves 6.

Rolled Rib Roast of Beef with Yorkshire Pudding

1 rolled rib roast of beef
salt and freshly ground black
pepper
1 teaspoon dry mustard

Yorkshire Pudding:
1 cup (125 g) flour
pinch of salt
1 large egg
1 cup (250 ml) milk
fat from the roast

1. Rub all the surfaces of the roast with the salt and pepper and dry mustard.
2. Place on a rack in a roasting pan and cook in a moderate oven 350°F (180°C) for 25 minutes per pound (55 minutes per 1 kg). Keep warm, after removing from the roasting pan.
3. Make a gravy from the pan drippings and cook Yorkshire Pudding.
4. Make a well in the center of the flour and salt mixed together. Break the egg into the well and gradually stir in the flour. Add half the milk gradually until a smooth batter is formed. Beat with the back of a spoon facing upwards for 10 minutes until bubbles form on the surface. Allow the batter to stand covered for 30 minutes.
5. Stir in the rest of the milk just before cooking.
6. Grease 12 muffin pans or 1 large cake pan with the fat from the roast and pour the batter into the pans or pan and cook in a very hot oven 450°F (230°C) for 20 minutes or until golden brown and puffed up and crispy.

Serves 6-8.

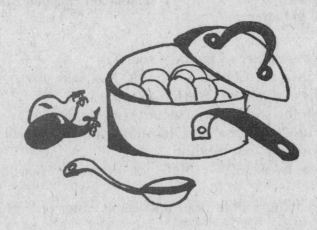

Quick Beef Curry

1½ lb (750 g) chuck steak
   (blade may be used)
1 large can curry paste (hot
   or mild according to taste)
1 large onion, chopped
1 large potato, chopped
flour, salt and pepper
oil

1. Cut the meat into 1 inch (2½ cm) cubes and roll in some seasoned flour and set aside.
2. Brown the onions in about 1 tablespoon oil until brown, add the floured beef and brown on all sides. Add the can of curry paste and the chopped potato. Cover and cook about 1 hour. Turn off and leave for about 1 hour. Return to low heat and cook again for a further 1 hour or until the meat is tender.

If the sauce is too thick it may be thinned by adding a little water.

Serves 4.

Mild Beef Curry

1½ lb (750 g) chuck steak or
   blade
2 tablespoons (40 g) butter
2 large onions, chopped
2 tablespoons curry powder
   (according to taste)
½ cup (125 ml) stock (made
   from a cube)

1 tablespoon lemon juice
½ teaspoon ground ginger
½ teaspoon ground cinnamon
   or 2 inch piece cinnamon stick
½ cup (125 ml) Coconut Milk
2 teaspoons salt

1. Cut steak into small cubes and brown on all sides in the butter in a fry-pan. Set meat aside.
2. Add a little more butter and the onion. Fry until soft and stir in the curry powder and cook for 3 minutes until the mixture is well browned.
3. Return the beef to the pan stirring well and lifting anything stuck to the bottom of the pan. Cover with the rest of the ingredients and cook again for 2 minutes. Simmer gently, covered tightly, for 1½ hours or until meat is tender and the sauce has thickened.

Serves 6.

Mediterranean Beef

1½ lb (750 g) round
   or blade steak
2 tablespoons oil
3 onions, chopped
3 cloves garlic, crushed
1½ cups chopped, skinned
   tomatoes
1 tablespoon tomato paste
1 bay leaf, crushed

3 whole cloves
1 cup (250 ml) red wine
1 teaspoon brown sugar
1 teaspoon basil
1 teaspoon salt
freshly ground black pepper
1 lb (500 g) boiled spaghetti
grated Parmesan cheese

1. Cut the beef into 1 inch (2½ cm) cubes and brown in hot oil on all sides. Lift out and set aside.
2. Saute the onions and garlic in the pan until soft, add tomatoes, tomato paste, wine, bay leaf, cloves, sugar, salt and pepper, return the beef to the pan and cover and simmer for 1½ hours. Serve with the boiled spaghetti and sprinkle with grated cheese.

Serves 4.

Alpine Steak

2 lb (1 kg) thick slice round steak
2 tablespoons (40 g) butter
2 onions, sliced
1 can tomatoes, chopped about
   14 oz (425 g)

1 tablespoon tomato sauce
1 teaspoon brown sugar
2 teaspoons Worcestershire sauce
salt and pepper

1. Slash the meat at intervals to prevent curling.
2. Brown the meat in some melted butter in a frypan. Reduce the heat and add onion slices. Cook until soft.
3. Add the tomatoes, tomato sauce, sugar, Worcestershire sauce and season to taste.
4. Cover tightly and simmer for 1½ hours or until the steak is tender.

Serve on a plate and pour the sauce over the slice to serve.

Serves 6.

French Beef Casserole

4 lb (2 kg) round steak (in one
  piece with fat removed)
veal knuckle, cut into chunks
4 oz (125 g) bacon fat
2 cloves garlic, slivered
½ cup (125 ml) dry red wine
4 sliced onions

8-12 baby carrots
1 teaspoon dried mixed herbs
1 bay leaf
12 whole peppercorns
1 teaspoon grated orange rind
2 large tomatoes, sliced
butter or table margarine

1. Cut incisions all over the piece of beef and push into these bacon fat and garlic slivers. Tie with string, rub with salt and pepper.
2. Melt some bacon fat, butter or good beef dripping in a heavy casserole with a very well-fitting lid. Brown the meat and pour off excess fat and swill dish gently with a little red wine to take up the meat flavor.
3. Replace meat in the casserole and surround with pieces of veal knuckle, cover with sliced onion, carrots.
4. Season with salt and pepper if needed and add the other seasonings, orange rind and sliced tomatoes.
5. Cover all the ingredients with half wine and half water and tightly seal the casserole. Perhaps some aluminum foil would help.
6. Cook either very slowly on top of the stove or place on the low shelf of the oven and cook for 7 or 8 hours at 300°F (150°C).
7. Cool then chill in refrigerator until beef sets in the jelly.

Serves 6-8.

Beef and Beer

2 lb (1 kg) stewing beef, chuck, round or blade	1¼ cups (300 ml) beer
3 tablespoons (60 g) butter	mixed herbs
2 large onions, chopped	1½ teaspoons salt
3 cloves garlic, crushed	freshly ground black pepper
2 tablespoons flour	nutmeg
	1 tablespoon brown sugar

1. Cut the meat into 1 inch (2½ cm) cubes and brown each side in the butter. When brown set aside.
2. Sauté onion until soft and garlic and cook a little longer. Stir in the flour and cook for a minute. Return the beef to the pan and pour in the beer. Stir constantly until the mixture thickens and begins to bubble. Add the rest of the ingredients, cover and simmer gently for 2 hours, until beef is tender. Adjust the seasoning and serve.

Serve with whole new potatoes or buttered noodles and a tossed salad.

Serves 4-6.

Scotch Eggs

1 lb (500 g) pork sausage meat	6 hard-boiled eggs
½ cup breadcrumbs	1 egg, beaten with 1 tablespoon water
1 egg	
1 tablespoon bottled barbecue sauce or tasty sauce	dry breadcrumbs
1 tablespoon flour	oil or fat for frying
salt and pepper	

1. Mix the pork sausage meat with the breadcrumbs, the egg and the sauce, season with salt and pepper and divide into 6 equal portions.
2. Add the seasonings and coat the eggs. Shape a portion of the sausage meat around each egg enclosing it completely. Brush with beaten egg and coat with crumbs.
3. Deep fry the scotch eggs for 5-7 minutes in hot but not too hot oil or fat until brown all over. Drain and serve whole or cut in half with tomato sauce and vegetables.

Serves 4-6.

Hamburgers

1½ lb (750 g) ground beef
1 onion, grated
1 teaspoon salt
¼ teaspoon pepper

1. Mix the ingredients together and shape into patties.
2. Cook either by broiling, pan frying in a little fat or cooking on a barbecue, 4 minutes each side.
3. Serve in a toasted hamburger bun with your favorite sauce, lettuce, tomato and raw or cooked onion rings.

Serves 4.

Variations:

Cheese burgers; Top the hamburger with sliced cheddar cheese and broil until cheese melts.

Pineapple burgers; Fry fresh or canned sliced pineapple in a little butter and put on the top of the hamburger.

Snowy burgers; Top with mashed potato and sprinkle with grated cheese and put under a broiler until cheese melts and potato browns.

Egg and Bacon burgers; Place a fried egg, cooked bacon and fried tomato on top of each hamburger.

Hamburgers with Cheese

1½ lb (750 g) ground beef
⅔ cup (166 ml) evaporated milk
1 egg
½ cup fine cracker crumbs
½ cup chopped green pepper

¼ cup chopped onions
1 tablespoon prepared mustard
salt and pepper
5 oz (155 g) soft cheese

1. Combined all the ingredients except the cheese.
2. Pat onto waxed paper spreading the mixture into a 12 inch square. Spread with the cheese. Roll the meat into a roll or loaf, seal the edges and cut 12, 1 inch (2½ cm) slices. Broil under a slow broiler for at least 16 minutes.

Serves 4.

Pot Roast with Macaroni

2½ lb (1¼ kg) rump roast
   in one piece
salt and pepper
1 tablespoon (20 g) butter
2 cups (500 ml) red wine
2 onions, chopped
2 bay leaves

6 peppercorns
½ cup fresh or sour cream
¾ lb (375 g) macaroni
1 tablespoon salt
6 cups (1500 ml) boiling water
1 tablespoon (20 g) butter

1. Rub the salt and pepper into the meat and fry in butter until the meat is brown all over. Remove and put into a large saucepan. Pour the wine into the frying pan, swill it around while it is still hot and pour over the meat.
2. Add the onions, bay leaves and peppercorns and cook over low heat for 1½ hours. The meat should be tender but not overcooked. Add the sour cream.
3. Meanwhile put the macaroni into 6 cups of boiling salted water, bring to the boil again, turn to a low heat and boil until tender, about 20 minutes. Strain and add butter.
4. To serve, cut the meat into slices and arrange on a dish and garnish with macaroni.

Serves 4-6.

Savory Ground Beef

4 lb (2 kg) ground beef	1 can 13 oz (425 g) fresh peeled
2 onions, chopped	tomatoes
2 tablespoons (40 g) butter or oil	1 cup (250 ml) of red wine
½ cup chopped celery	salt and pepper
1 can 13 oz (425 g) tomato soup	1 teaspoon basil

1. Sauté the onion in oil until just starting to brown; add the meat and cook until it browns.
2. Add the soup, celery, tomatoes, wine and seasonings. Cover and simmer for 30 minutes.

Makes 8 cups.

This ground beef sauce is used for toast toppers.
Other variations are:
Potato Pie; Top with mashed potato and dot with cheese and butter. Cook in oven until the potato is brown and cheese melted.
Spaghetti Bolognaise; Add some garlic to the mixture and serve over the boiled spaghetti with a sprinkling of Parmesan cheese.
Chilli con carne; Add a chopped green pepper, some chilli powder and some red kidney beans.

Beef Rolls

1 slice of blade steak per person	butter
salt and pepper	4 tablespoons white wine
mustard, dry	1 tablespoon flour
1 slice bacon per person, chopped	2 tablespoons sour cream
onion, finely chopped	chopped parsley

1. Cut the beef into thin slices and flatten with a mallet.
2. Sprinkle the beef with salt, pepper and dry mustard. Spread the beef with chopped bacon, a little of the chopped onion and some chopped parsley. Roll up and secure with a toothpick.
3. Sauté some chopped onion in butter until soft and sauté the rolls in this until brown on all sides.
4. Remove the onions and beef and place in a casserole dish. Cover with wine and cook in the oven for about 1 hour.
5. When the rolls are cooked, remove and keep warm. Add sour cream to the sauce and thicken with some flour. Return the rolls and heat through.

Meat Pie

1 pkt of frozen pie pastry
1 lb (500 g) ground beef
tomato juice, soup or purée
1 onion, chopped
salt and pepper
curry powder

1. Brown the onions, add the meat and cook until just done.
2. Add the soup, sauce or puréed tomatoes, curry powder and season.
3. Line pie plate with rolled out pie pastry and fill it with the meat mixture. Cover the top with pastry. Make little slits in the top of the pastry to allow steam to escape.

Serves 4.

Golden Meat Pie

1 cup soft breadcrumbs	½ cup chopped onion
½ cup (125 ml) milk	2 tablespoons (40 g) butter
1 lb (500 g) ground beef	1 package frozen corn
1 beaten egg	1 cup of canned tomatoes, strained
2 tablespoons grated onion	1 teaspoon salt
1 teaspoon salt	½ teaspoon basil
1 tablespoon Worcestershire sauce	1 tablespoon Parmesan cheese
3 tablespoons tomato or plum sauce	½ cup chopped crispy cooked bacon

1. Heat oven to 350°F (180°C).
2. Soften breadcrumbs in milk, add meat, egg, onion, season with salt and pepper and mix well. Line the bottom and sides of a pie dish with the mixture and bake in the oven for 45 minutes.
3. Cook ¼ cup of chopped onions in butter until brown and add the rest of the ingredients and simmer for 15 minutes. Fill the meat crust with this mixture and return to the oven to heat through.
4. Garnish with parsley.

Serves 4-6.

Sausage Rolls

500 g (1 lb) finely ground pork
1 small onion, grated
1 tablespoon finely chopped parsley
1 tablespoon tomato sauce
1 package about 11 oz (345 g) of
   prepared puff pastry

1. Mix ground pork with the onion and parsley and add the tomato sauce.
2. Divide into 4 portions. Shape each portion into a long roll and roll on a lightly floured surface.
3. Roll the pastry out thinly and cut into 4 strips, 5 inches (12 cm) wide and as long as the rolls of ground pork. Place a roll of sausage toward one end of the pastry strip, moisten the lower edge with water. Roll sausage and pastry over to enclose meat completely with pastry.
4. Place the rolls in a greased baking dish, seam-side down, glaze with a little milk or egg beaten with milk. Put three slits on top and bake in a hot oven 450°F (230°C) for 15 minutes, lower heat and cook a further 10-15 minutes at 375°F (190°C).

Serves 4.

Meat Ball Stroganoff

2 lb (1 kg) finely ground beef
2 eggs
1 large onion, grated
½ cup dry breadcrumbs
½ teaspoon ground allspice
salt and pepper
oil for frying

1 cup (250 ml) beef stock
 (use beef cube and water)
pinch nutmeg
8 oz (250 g) mushrooms, sliced
1 tablespoon flour
½ cup cream
1 tablespoon lemon juice

1. Mix thoroughly ground beef, beaten eggs, onion, dry breadcrumbs, allspice, salt and pepper and shape into balls the size of a walnut.
2. Brown the meat balls in the oil in a frying pan. Set aside and drain off all but 2 tablespoons of the oil and saute mushrooms.
3. Add the stock and nutmeg and season to taste. Pour over the meat balls and cover and cook slowly for 45 minutes.
4. Thicken the sauce with a little flour mixed to a paste with some cold water. Cook for another minute and when sauce bubbles stir in a mixture of the lemon juice and cream. Heat again but do not boil.

Serve with buttered noodles and tossed green salad.

Serves 4-6.

Glazed Beef Loaf

2 lb (1 kg) ground beef
1 cup dry breadcrumbs
4 tablespoons grated onion
1 tablespoon chopped parsley
salt and pepper
1 cup sour cream

2 eggs
2 tablespoons Worcestershire sauce
½ cup tomato or Plum Sauce
 (see recipe)
1½ tablespoons corn syrup or honey
1 teaspoon Worcestershire sauce

1. Mix the first 8 ingredients together very well. Shape into a loaf or pack into a greased loaf pan and bake in a moderate oven 350°F (180°C) for 45 to 50 minutes.
2. If loaf is baked in a loaf pan, turn out onto a baking sheet and glaze with a mixture of the tomato or Plum Sauce, corn syrup or honey and Worcestershire sauce. If the loaf is standing free in a baking dish just pour the glaze straight over the loaf. Bake again for about 20 minutes.

Serves 4-6.

Cabbage Rolls

1 medium sized cabbage
water
1½ lb (750 g) finely ground beef
1 cup boiled rice
½ cup chopped onion
1 tablespoon (20 g) butter

salt and pepper
2 tablespoons (40 g) butter
1 cup (250 ml) of white wine
 or beef stock
1 cup sour cream

1. Cut the outside leaves from the cabbage and remove the core from the head so that the water can get to the leaves more easily. Put the cabbage upside down in enough boiling water to fill and cover the cabbage. Boil for 10 minutes and drain. When cool enough, detach the leaves and trim off any thick center veins.
2. Sauté the onions in 1 tablespoon butter until soft but not brown and mix with the meat, boiled rice, salt and pepper. Put 1 or 2 tablespoons, depending on the size of the leaves, on the thicker part of the leaves and fold in three sides, then roll up.
3. Heat the 2 tablespoons butter in a pan and fry the rolls very quickly on all sides. Put in a saucepan and pour over the wine or stock.
4. Cover and bring to boil, reduce and simmer for 1 hour. Add more liquid if necessary. When cooked pour over the sour cream and simmer for another 5 minutes. Thicken the sauce with a little cornstarch if necessary.

Serves 4-6.

Beef Mexicana

2 onions, chopped
2 cloves garlic, chopped
2 tablespoons (40 g) butter or oil
1½ lb (750 g) ground beef
1 teaspoon tomatoes, chopped
3 tablespoons tomato sauce
salt and pepper

1 cup (250 ml) water
1 cup (250 ml) white wine
¼ cup (60 g) raw rice
1 cup fresh or frozen peas or
 sliced beans
1 cup canned or frozen corn
chopped parsley

1. Sauté the onion and garlic in butter and when soft add the ground beef. When the beef is brown add chilli powder, tomatoes, tomato sauce, water, wine, salt and pepper to taste. Cover and simmer for 15 minutes.
2. Stir in the rice and vegetables, bring to the boil, reduce heat, cover and simmer for about 20 minutes or until the rice is tender. Sprinkle with chopped parsley before serving.

Serves 6.

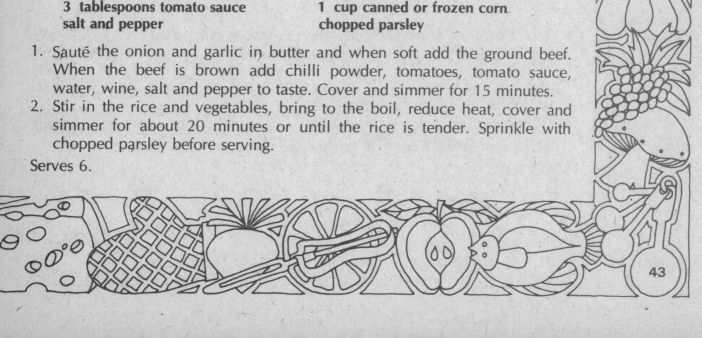

Curried Meat Balls

1 onion, chopped	1½ cups (375 ml) water
3 tablespoons oil	2 lb (1 kg) ground beef
3 tablespoons curry powder	or veal
⅓ teaspoon coriander	2 slices bread
⅓ teaspoon cumin seed	a little water
⅓ teaspoon ginger	salt and pepper
⅓ teaspoon mustard	1 small cup currants, steamed
¼ teaspoon cloves	2 tablespoons coconut
¼ teaspoon mace	2 teaspoons grated lemon peel
2 cloves garlic, crushed	fluffy rice
1 can tomato purée	

1. Brown the onion in the oil in a heavy frying pan.
2. Mix the curry, coriander, cumin seed, ginger, mustard, cloves, mace, garlic in ¼ cup water to make a thin paste. Add to the onion and cook until brown. Do not burn.
3. Add the tomato purée and water and mix until smooth. Season to taste.
4. Crumble the bread in a little water. Squeeze out and mix the minced beef or veal. Season and make into 24 meat balls. Brown these in a little oil and add to the sauce.
5. Cover the pan and simmer for 1 hour. Serve with boiled rice, mixed with currants, coconut and lemon peel.

Makes 24 meat balls.

Fried Meat Turnovers

2 cups 1 lb (500 g) Savory Ground Beef (see recipe)	½ teaspoon salt
3 cups (375 g) flour	½ cup (125 g) butter or margarine
2 teaspoons baking powder	⅔ cup (166 ml) milk

1. Sift the flour, baking powder and salt into a bowl. Melt the butter and pour into the flour with milk and mix to make a firm dough. Roll out thinly. Cut into rounds about 4 inch (10 cm). Brush edges with milk or water and place a tablespoon of meat mixture into the center of each round. Fold over and press the edges to seal completely.
2. Deep fry in hot oil 3 or 4 at a time for 1 minute turning once to brown evenly. Lift out and drain and serve hot.

Serves 4.

Beef and Kidney Loaf

1½ lb (750 g) ground beef
(topside)
1 lb (500 g) sheep or ox kidney,
ground
4 bacon slices, chopped
2 onions, chopped finely

¾ cup dry breadcrumbs or
cereal crumbs
½ cup chopped raisins
salt and pepper
2 eggs
½ cup grated Cheddar cheese

1. Combine all the ingredients except the cheese and mix well until blended.
2. Grease a loaf pan and dust lightly with extra crumbs. Press half the mixture into the pan and sprinkle with grated cheese and top with the remaining mixture, press down firmly.
3. Bake in a moderate oven 375°F (190°C) for 1 hour. Pour any juices from the pan into an open oven dish and unmold the loaf into the dish. Return to the oven for a further ½ hour, basting with the meat juices and until the meat is nicely brown.

The loaf may be made without a loaf pan by shaping into two smaller loaves and brushing top with oil or melted butter and baking in a moderate oven for 1½ hours.

Serves 4-6.

Chilli Con Carne

3 large onions, sliced
1 lb (500 g) ground chuck
1 tablespoon chilli powder (less
if desired)
1 bay leaf, crushed
1 teaspoon oregano

1 large can whole tomatoes
2 cans kidney beans, drained
1 clove garlic, crushed
1 tablespoon brown sugar
1 tablespoon tomato sauce
2 teaspoons soya sauce

1. Sauté the chopped onion in the butter until soft but not brown.
2. Remove the onions from the pan and add a little more butter and fry the ground meat until brown. Sprinkle on the chili powder, add the bay leaf, oregano, salt and pepper if desired. Simmer for 7 minutes and add the tomatoes, garlic, brown sugar, tomato sauce and soya sauce. Simmer again for 3 minutes.
3. Turn into a casserole dish and mix in the onions and cook in 400°F (200°C) oven for 1 hour.

Serves 4.

45

Glazed Corned Beef

corned beef
1 teaspoon mustard
1 cup (250 ml) beer, ginger ale
   or vinegar
1 apple stuck with cloves
1 onion
1 cup marmalade

1. Place corned beef in heavy pan, add the mustard, liquid apple and onion.
2. Cook slowly for about 1 hour per pound or until done.
3. Leave the meat to stand in the liquid overnight in the refrigerator.
4. Place in a baking dish and cover with a thin layer of butter or fat and bake very slowly for about 1 hour, 250°F (120°C).
5. During the last hour of the cooking, glaze with the marmalade and cook until glazed, basting frequently.

Serves 6-8.

Corned Beef with Vegetables

1 piece corned beef brisket
   3 lb-4 b (1½ kg-2 kg)
1 onion, quartered
12 whole peppercorns
1 carrot, sliced
1 stalk celery, chopped

1 bay leaf
4 medium carrots, quartered
8 small onions, whole
8 medium potatoes
6-8 wedges of cabbage

1. Rinse the corned beef in cold water and cover with warm water in a large saucepan. Add the onion, peppercorns, one carrot, celery, and bay leaf, bring to boil and simmer for 1½ hours.
2. Lift out the beef, strain the stock and return both the stock and the beef to the saucepan and add the 4 carrots and onions. Cook for another hour.
3. Add the potatoes and cabbage and cook a further 30 minutes. Serve on a platter with the vegetables surrounding the meat. Thicken the stock if necessary. You can also make a white, parsley or onion and mustard sauce. You can also use a little of the stock from the meat in your white sauce.

Serves 6-8.

Spiced Corned Silverside with Fruit Glaze

1 piece corned beef brisket, cooked (uncooked 4 lb (2 kg))	½ cup brown sugar
whole cloves	½ teaspoon ground allspice
½ cup (125 ml) orange or pineapple juice	½ teaspoon ground ginger

1. Cook the beef by washing well in cold water and placing in a large saucepan and covering with warm water. Add whole peppercorns, 1 sliced onion, bay leaf and simmer for about 1½ hours until almost tender. Do not boil. Leave the meat in the liquid to cool. Lift out and drain. Reserve the stock.
2. When nearly cooled score the fat in a criss cross pattern and stud each cross with a whole clove. Add ½ cup (125 ml) of the stock from the meat to the rest of the ingredients, cook for about 2 minutes and pour over the corned beef. Place in a slow oven 325°F (160°C) and bake for 1 hour, basting meat regularly during the cooking with pan juices.

Serves 6-8.

This is nice served with potatoes baked in their jackets and sour cream on top together with baked pineapple slices, glazed carrots and glazed onions.

Tongue in Breadcrumbs

- 1 ox tongue
- 1 egg
- 1 cup breadcrumbs
- 2 tablespoons (60 g) butter
- 1 tablespoon oil
- 1 tablespoon chopped parsley

1. Put the tongue into a saucepan of cold water, bring to the boil, cover and simmer until the tongue is tender. Add salt if tongue is not salted.
2. When cool, remove the skin and cut into slices ½ inch (1 cm) thick.
3. Dip the slices into the beaten egg, and then breadcrumbs and fry in the hot butter and oil.

Serves 4.

Pressed Beef Tongue

1 corned beef tongue	some mixed herbs
2 onions, sliced	1 bay leaf
2 carrots, sliced	6 peppercorns
1 stalk celery, chopped	

1. Wash the tongue well and soak for 2 hours. Place in a deep saucepan and cover completely with cold water. Add the rest of the ingredients and cook slowly for 3 hours after bringing it to the boil.
2. Lift out and cool to remove the skin and trim off the root. Place in a deep round dish or cake tin. Add just enough of the strained stock to just come halfway up the tongue and cover with a plate. Place a weight on top and chill in the refrigerator for 24 hours. Turn out of the mold, slice and serve.

Serves 4-6.

Lamb tongue may be prepared in the same way. Use 6 tongues for the above recipe and cook for half the time.

Tripe Yugoslavia

2 lb (1 kg) tripe	2 tablespoons chopped parsley
2 lb (1 kg) onions, chopped	1 teaspoon basil
2 lb (1 kg) tomatoes, chopped	parsley
4 slices bacon, chopped	salt
1 lb (500 g) potatoes, cubed	oil or butter
2 cloves garlic, crushed	

1. Cut the tripe into fine slices.
2. Heat the oil or butter in a heavy frying pan and cook the onion, garlic and parsley until soft but not brown.
3. Add the tripe and half the tomatoes and cook until the tripe is tender. Add the rest of the ingredients and cook until the potatoes are just done. Thicken with a little cornstarch if desired.

Serves 6.

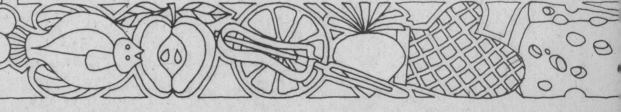

Oxtail Plaka Style

2 oxtails
3 tablespoons olive
3 cloves garlic, crushed
6 tablespoons brandy
1 large glass red wine
1 large onion, grated

1 tablespoon chopped parsley
stock
grated lemon rind from 1 lemon
grated orange rind from 1 orange
black olives, stoned and sliced

1. Cut the oxtail into pieces. Heat the oil in a heavy casserole and fry the oxtail gently for about 2 minutes each side, together with the garlic. Pour the brandy over the tail and set alight. When the flames have finished add the wine, and just enough stock to cover the tail. Add the onion, orange and lemon rind, cover and simmer for 3 hours at 250°F (120°C). Let stand for 3 hours.
2. Skim the fat from the casserole, add the black olives and cook for a further 1 hour.

Serves 6.

Hungarian Oxtail Ragout

2 oxtails
½ cup sliced celery
2 large onions, chopped
mixed herbs
1½ cups (375 ml) red wine
1 teaspoon salt
freshly ground black pepper

1 tablespoon brown sugar
3 tablespoons (60 g) butter
or margarine
3 tablespoons flour
2 teaspoons paprika
2 cloves garlic, crushed
1 cup tomato purée

1. Cut the oxtail into thick slices, wash and dry.
2. Mix celery, carrot, onion, herbs, wine, salt, pepper and sugar in a bowl and add oxtails. Marinate for at least 3 hours.
3. Drain the oxtails and coat with flour and brown in the butter in a pan with a cover. Stir in the remaining flour, paprika, garlic, tomato purée. Stir until thick, lower heat and simmer for 2½ hours or until oxtail is tender. Skim off the fat, adjust seasoning and serve with buttered noodles sprinkled with poppy seeds.

Serves 6.

Veal

Roasted Veal with Mushrooms

4 lb (2 kg) veal shoulder or other cuts of roasting veal	3 tablespoons (60 g) butter ⅓ cup flour
1 lb (500 g) mushrooms	2 oz (60 g) grated cheese
bay leaf	1 teaspoon mustard
onion	salt
mace	pepper
8 peppercorns	½ teaspoon nutmeg
1¼ pints (600 ml) milk	1 tablespoon lemon juice

1. Roast the veal for 2 hours and cut into slices about ½ inch (1 cm) thick.
2. Put the mushrooms in a saucepan and cook in a little butter until soft. Put through a sieve.
3. Make a sauce by putting the bay leaf, onion, peppercorns, mace into the milk and cook over a low heat for 10 minutes. Melt the butter, add the flour and make a smooth paste. Mix the flavored milk in slowly, after straining, mix quickly and keep sauce smooth. Simmer for 3 minutes and season.
4. Add the sieved mushrooms to 1½ cups (375 ml) of the sauce you have just made and season with nutmeg, lemon juice and if necessary salt and pepper.
5. In an oven proof dish place the slices of veal and spread with the mushroom mixture.
6. Take the rest of the white sauce and beat into it the cheese (leave about 2 tablespoons to sprinkle on top), mustard and if necessary salt and pepper. Now pour this cheese sauce over the slices of meat covered in the mushroom sauce. Sprinkle with the rest of the grated cheese and brown in the oven.

This dish can be made some hours ahead and heated when necessary.

Serves 6-8.

Rolled Shoulder of Veal with Fruity Rice Stuffing

1 shoulder of veal, boned
salt and pepper
Fruity Rice Stuffing (see recipe)
butter
½ cup (125 ml) dry white wine

1. Open the veal shoulder out and season with salt and pepper. Spread generously with the Fruity Rice Stuffing, roll up and fasten with skewers or string. Rub again on the outside with salt and pepper.
2. Spread with some butter (bacon fat may be used) and cook in a baking dish in an oven 350°F (180°C) for 45 minutes per pound (90 minutes per 1 kg) or if using a meat thermometer it should read 170°F (75°C). Baste regularly during cooking.
3. When cooked place aside and make a gravy from the drippings in the pan with the wine added.

Serves 4-6.

Veal Roast

5 lb (2½ kg) veal rump	bay leaf
garlic	¼ cup flour
salt and pepper	1 grated onion
allspice	2 stalks of celery, chopped
thyme and sage	4 sliced carrots

1. Firstly, rub the meat with garlic and then sprinkle on a mixture of flour, salt, pepper, spices and herbs.
2. Brown the meat in some hot fat, remove, then brown the vegetables. Return the meat to the baking dish and add about 1 cup (250 ml) of boiling water.
3. Cook slowly until tender about 2 to 2½ hours.
4. Thicken the juices from the meat to make a gravy.

Serves 6.

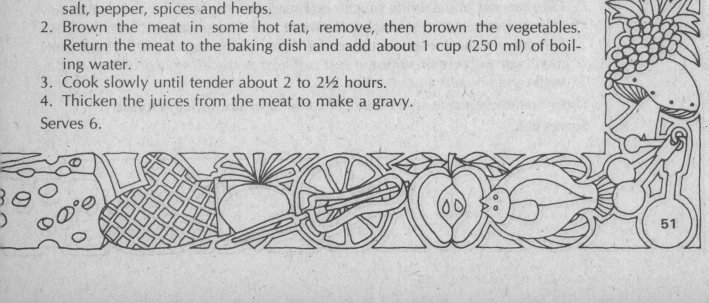

Veal with Bacon and Herb Stuffing

1 heel of round of veal
2 tablespoons (40 g) butter
salt and freshly ground black
    pepper

½ teaspoon paprika
8 oz (250 g) bacon slices
Bacon and Herb Stuffing (see
    recipe)

1. Cut a deep pocket in the veal. Fill with the Bacon and Herb Stuffing to which ½ teaspoon sage has been added. Secure with skewers.
2. Place the veal in a baking dish and rub all the surfaces with a mixture of the salt and pepper and paprika. Place the bacon over the veal and cook in a moderate oven 350°F (180°C) for 45 minutes per pound (90 minutes per 1 kg). If you have a meat thermometer it should read 170°F (75°C). Baste several times during the cooking. Remove the bacon at the last 25 minutes so as to allow the veal to brown evenly.
3. Drain the fat from the pan and make a gravy from the drippings.

Serves 6.

Wiener Schnitzel

2 lb (1 kg) veal steak, ½ inch
    (1 cm) thick
lemon juice
salt and pepper
2 eggs, beaten

4 tablespoons cold milk
4 tablespoons flour
fine dry breadcrumbs
oil for frying

1. Cut the veal into serving pieces and marinate the veal in about 4 tablespoons lemon juice for at least 1 hour at room temperature.
2. Dip the veal into seasoned flour, then into beaten eggs with the milk and then coat with breadcrumbs.
3. Fry in the oil until a golden brown.

Some grated cheese can be added to the breadcrumbs to add flavor.

Serves 4.

Schnitzel Traudy Style

6 veal steaks about ½ inch (1 cm) thick	egg
6 slices bacon	milk
6 slices Swiss cheese	oil
salt and pepper	breadcrumbs
	oil to fry

1. Cook the slices of bacon under a broiler until just done.
2. Lay the bacon and cheese on top of the veal steaks and sprinkle with salt and pepper. Make a roll and tuck in ends of veal.
3. Mix egg, milk and a dash of oil together and dip the veal rolls into the mixture and then coat with breadcrumbs.
4. Fry until golden brown.

This is delicious served with boiled cauliflower dipped in the egg and breadcrumbs and fried the same way as the veal.

Serves 6.

Veal Escalopes with Ham and Cheese

4 slices veal steak, flattened	2 tablespoons (40 g) butter
salt and pepper	1 tablespoon oil
3 tablespoons flour	4 slices ham
1 egg	4 slices Swiss cheese
dry breadcrumbs	
1 tablespoon grated Parmesan cheese	

1. Mix the salt and pepper with flour. Beat the egg with the water and mix the crumbs with the grated cheese. Dip the steaks firstly into the flour, then into the egg mixture and then coat thoroughly with the cheese and breadcrumb mixture, pressing them into the steaks firmly.
2. Heat the butter and oil in a pan and fry the veal over a moderate heat until golden brown and thoroughly cooked. Drain on absorbent paper.
3. Top each steak with 1 slice of ham, then 1 slice of cheese and place under a hot broiler until the cheese melts.

Serves 4.

Veal in Vermouth

2 lb (1 kg) veal, cut very thin
2 cloves garlic
flour
salt and pepper
½ cup (125 g) butter

small can of button mushrooms
½ cup (125 ml) dry vermouth
lemon juice
finely chopped parsley

1. Cut the steak into serving pieces. Rub with garlic and roll in seasoned flour.
2. Melt some butter in a pan and brown the veal on both sides.
3. Add the mushrooms and vermouth. Cook for 20 minutes or until tender. Sprinkle with lemon juice and parsley and serve.

Serves 4.

Veal Rolls with Wine

4 pieces of veal (cutlets may be used)
4 slices bacon
juice of 1 lemon
flour for dusting
½ cup grated cheese
salt and pepper

2 tablespoons (40 g) butter
1 large onion, chopped
1 clove garlic, crushed
2 dessertspoons flour
1 cup (250 ml) white wine
capers or thyme

1. Flatten the veal steaks. Rub each piece of meat with lemon juice and roll in a mixture of the flour and grated cheese.
2. Place each steak on a slice of bacon and roll up, bacon on the outside. Secure with a toothpick.
3. Melt the butter in a frying pan and brown onion and garlic, remove and put aside the onion and in the same pan brown the veal rolls on all sides. Place in a casserole.
4. Blend 2 dessertspoons flour in the pan and brown lightly, add the wine and stir until it is smooth and boils. Return the onion and garlic to the pan and mix in 1 tablespoon of capers or thyme. Pour over the veal rolls, cover and bake in a moderate oven 350°F (180°C) for 1 hour.

Serves 4.

Veal Curry with Brazil Nuts

1½ lb (750 g) veal steak	½ cup yoghurt
flour	1 tablespoon curry powder
salt and pepper	pepper
1 tablespoon oil	thyme
1 cup onions, grated	marjoram
1 can mushroom soup	½ cup brazil nuts

1. Cut the veal into 1 inch (2½ cm) cubes, roll in seasoned flour and saute in the oil in a heavy pan.
2. Add the grated onions and cook until soft.
3. Remove the onions and meat to a casserole and add the can of mushroom soup and yoghurt to the pan. Mix together, add the curry and herbs and nuts and heat, quickly. Pour over the meat in the casserole and bake in a moderate 350°F (180°C) oven for 45 minutes.

Serves 4.

Veal Steak with Pork Filling

4 veal steaks	½ cup tomato purée
1 lb (500 g) ground pork	salt and pepper
¼ lb (125 g) chopped bacon	½ teaspoon nutmeg
½ lb (250 g) button mushrooms	½ cup sour cream
3 tablespoons butter	½ teaspoon salt
½ cup chopped onions	1 cup (250 ml) white wine

1. Flatten the steaks and sprinkle with salt and pepper.
2. Slice the mushrooms and sauté in some butter. Mix with the ground pork and chopped bacon, blend well and divide into 4 portions and place each portion in the center of each piece of veal, roll up and secure with a toothpick.
3. Heat the rest of the butter in a frying pan, brown the rolls on all sides, put aside. Fry the onions in the pan and add the tomato purée and wine. Bring this to the boil.
4. Place the rolls in a deep saucepan side by side in a row and pour the wine stock over them. Cover and simmer for 35 minutes. When ready to serve, the sauce may be thickened with a little cornstarch and served over the rolls.

Serve with boiled rice.

Serves 4.

Veal Goulash

2 lb (1 kg) boneless veal
3 tablespoons (60 g) butter
6 tablespoons brandy
4 tablespoons (80 g) butter
2 cups of grated carrot, celery and onion
2 tablespoons paprika
3 tablespoons flour

2 tablespoons tomato purée or 1 tablespoon tomato paste
2 cups chicken stock (use a chicken cube)
salt and pepper
1 cup sour cream
noodles, butter and caraway seeds

1. Cut the veal into 1 inch (2½ cm) cubes and brown in 3 tablespoons of the butter. Flame with the brandy and remove the meat.
2. Put another 4 tablespoons butter in the pan and sauté the mixed grated vegetables for 2 minutes. Mix in the paprika, sprinkle with flour, mix and stir in the tomato purée.
3. Stir in the stock slowly and mix until smooth. Bring to boil and season. Add the sour cream and put the veal back into the pan. Cover and simmer for 40 minutes or until the meat is tender.
4. Meanwhile cook the noodles in boiling salted water. Drain and toss with butter and 1 teaspoon caraway seeds.

Serves 4.

Brandied Kidneys

2 veal or 4 sheep kidneys
bacon fat
1 onion, chopped
4 tablespoons mushrooms, chopped

butter
salt and pepper
4 tablespoons cream
3 tablespoons brandy
parsley

1. Remove the membrane and fat from the kidneys and slice thinly.
2. Melt the bacon fat and fry the kidney pieces for 2 minutes. Add onions, mushrooms, butter (about 1 teaspoon), salt and pepper and cook for 7 minutes.
3. Add the cream and parsley and pour over the warmed brandy, set alight. Shake the pan until the flame dies and serve immediately.

Serves 4.

Veal Knuckle Pie

2 lb (1 kg) meat from knuckle
  of veal
the bone
1 tablespoon parsley
1 teaspoon thyme

1 small onion, grated
salt and pepper
½ lb (500 g) chopped bacon
pastry

1. Take the meat from the bone and put the bone in a saucepan, cover with water, parsley, thyme and onion and simmer for at least 2 hours.
2. Remove the bone and put the chopped meat and bacon in and cook until tender. Cool.
3. Meanwhile roll out pastry and cover the bottom of a pie dish. When the meat is cool, place the meat with sufficient thickened, seasoned, stock to keep moist, in the bottom of the pie dish. Cover with more pastry and bake until the pastry is cooked and golden brown.

This can be served hot or cold.

Serves 4.

Veal Birds with Raisins

4 lb (2 kg) veal steak cut into
  about 12 pieces
1 cup chopped seeded raisin
3 cups fresh breadcrumbs
2 tablespoons finely chopped
  parsley
1 tablespoon of grated lemon
  rind

1 tablespoon lemon juice
salt and pepper
3 tablespoons (60 g) melted butter
2 beaten eggs
salt and pepper
1 lb (500 g) bacon slices

1. Combine the raisins, breadcrumbs, parsley, lemon rind, lemon juice, salt and pepper, butter and eggs. Mix well and place in the center of each veal piece, roll up and secure with a toothpick.
2. Put into a baking dish with a little melted butter and sprinkle with a little salt and pepper.
3. Bake for 1 hour in a moderate oven 375°F (190°C) or until tender.
4. Place the bacon slices on top of each roll and bake for a further 15 minutes. Remove the rolls and keep warm. Thicken the meat drippings with flour if required. Pour over the meat rolls when serving.

Serves 6.

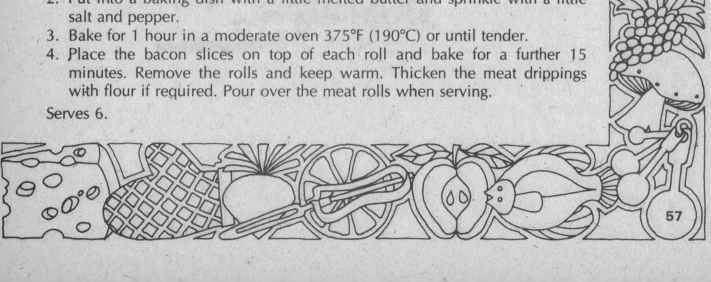

Blanquette of Veal

2 lb (1 kg) stewing veal, cut thickly
3 tablespoons (60 g) butter
1 onion, studded with 3 cloves
2 carrots, sliced
1½ cups (375 ml) stock, made with a cube
1 bay leaf, crushed
dash of rosemary, marjoram, sage
1 teaspoon salt
pepper
12 small onions, par boiled
4 oz (250 g) button mushrooms sautéed in butter and lemon juice or
1 small can button mushrooms
2 tablespoons flour
2 egg yolks
½ cup cream
pinch nutmeg

1. Cut the veal into cubes and soak in cold water and dry well after about 1 hour.
2. Melt 1 tablespoon of butter in a pan and fry the veal in it but do not brown, add the onion with the cloves, carrots, stock, salt and pepper, bay leaf and the mixed herbs. Cover and bring to the boil, skim and cover and cook for about 45 minutes.
3. Remove the veal and carrots. Strain the liquid and put aside. Clean the pan and melt the rest of the butter, add the flour and mix in the stock slowly until the sauce thickens. Add the veal pieces, carrots, whole onions and mushrooms. Cover and simmer, stirring regularly for 30 minutes or until the meat is tender.
4. Mix egg yolk, cream and nutmeg together and pour into veal mixture. Reheat but do not boil.

Serves 6.

Mixed Meat Rolls

1 lb (500 g) ground beef
1 lb (500 g) ground veal
½ lb (250 g) ground pork
1 medium onion, chopped
1 teaspoon salt
1 teaspoon pepper
1 clove garlic, crushed
1 teaspoon basil
dash of Worcestershire sauce
1 beaten egg

Pastry:
1 cup (125 g) flour
1 cup (250 g) butter
sherry to mix
chopped parsley

1. Break the butter through the flour with a knife and mix in enough sherry to make a firm dough. Add the parsley and roll out in long strips 8 inches (12 cm) wide and as thin as possible.
2. Combine meats, onion and seasonings, beaten egg and mix until they are all well blended.
3. Shape the mixture into rolls 5 inches (12 cm) long and 1½ inches (4 cm) in diameter and place on the pastry and carefully roll it around the meat. Cut and press the ends with a fork and place on an oven tray seam side down. Prick the top of the crust with a fork and cook in a 375°F (190°C) oven until they are golden brown.

Makes about 16 rolls.

Jellied Veal Loaf

3 cups ground veal
2 cups diced celery
4 tablespoons chopped parsley
1 tablespoon chopped chives
½ cup chopped sweet pickles
2 beef stock cubes, dissolved in
2 cups (500 ml) boiling water
2 bay leaves
3 peppercorns

marjoram
thyme
1½ tablespoons (22 g) gelatin
¼ cup (62½ ml) cold water
salt and pepper
3 tablespoons vinegar
Tabasco sauce
paprika
4 hard-boiled eggs, chopped

1. Mix the veal, celery, parsley, chives and pickles together.
2. Dissolve the beef cubes in the boiling water and add bay leaves, peppercorns, marjoram and thyme and simmer for 20 minutes.
3. Soak the gelatin in the cold water and dissolve it in the beef stock mixture and add to the veal mixture. Season with salt and pepper, vinegar, paprika and Tabasco sauce. Mix well and add the chopped eggs.
4. Pour into an oiled bread tin 9½ inches (24 cm) by 5½ inches (14 cm) by 3 inches (7 cm). Chill for several hours or until set.

Serves 10.

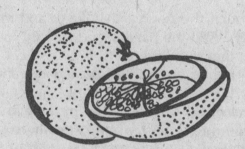

Lamb

Chops Mexican Style

1½ lb (750 g) lamb leg chops
2 teaspoons butter or oil
2 large onions, sliced
4 oz (125 g) uncooked rice
2 teaspoons salt
pepper
1 can peeled, canned tomatoes

1 tablespoon brown sugar
2 teaspoons Worcestershire sauce
1 beef cube
1 teaspoon soya sauce
1¾ cups (450 ml) water
paprika

1. Heat 2 teaspoons of butter or oil in a casserole.
2. Add the onion, rice, salt and pepper, tomatoes and sugar.
3. Mix together Worcestershire sauce, beef cube, soya sauce and paprika with the water and pour over the rest of the ingredients. Add the chops.
4. Cook in a moderate oven 350°F (180°C) for about 1 hour or until the chops are tender.

Serves 4-6.

Chops with Coconut

lamb chops (veal may also
   be used)
egg
coconut
salt and pepper
2 tablespoons (40 g) fat, butter
   or oil

1. Heat the fat in a baking dish.
2. Dip chops in seasoned egg and then in the coconut.
3. Place chops in the hot fat in a moderate oven 350°F (180°C).
4. Baste regularly and serve when chops are crisp.

Hawaiian Hotpot

2 lb (1 kg) lamb chops
fresh pineapple, sliced
8 oz (250 g) can tomato purée
1 medium can mushrooms
scallions
mixed herbs
red or white wine

1. Line the bottom of an ovenproof dish with some of the chops. Lay the pineapple slices on top of the chops and continue the layers, sprinkling mixed herbs and salt and pepper in between each layer.
2. Pour the tomato purée and mushrooms over the chops and sprinkle more herbs and the scallions on the top.
3. Pour enough wine over the dish so the liquid just reaches the last layer. Cook slowly until meat is done.

Serve with rice or mashed potatoes.

Serves 4-6.

Japanese Broiled Lamb

8 rib chops or cutlets
1 onion chopped,
   or scallions chopped
¼ cup soya sauce
¼ cup stock
finely sliced ginger root, fresh
   or canned

1. Put the onions or scallions, soya sauce and stock into a saucepan and boil for 1 minute. Cool and pour over the chops and let stand at least 8 hours.
2. Drain and broil under a preheated, moderate broiler, basting with the marinade and turning regularly, until done.

Serves 4-6.

Lamb Chops in Cheese Jackets

4 lamb cutlets or rib chops
flour
salt and pepper
1 egg
1 tablespoon water
½ cup grated hard cheese

¾ cup breadcrumbs
4 tablespoons oil
4 tablespoons tomato sauce
dash Tabasco sauce
1 teaspoon soya sauce
4 thin slices of cheese

1. Roll the chops in a mixture of the flour and salt and pepper. Dip in the egg mixed with the water and toss in a mixture of breadcrumbs and cheese.
2. Heat the oil in a frying pan until it is not quite smoking. Brown the chops on each side.
3. In a shallow pan mix tomato sauce soya sauce and a dash of Tabasco sauce. Roll the cutlets in this mixture and spread over the cutlets the slices of cheese.
4. Cook in a slow oven until the cheese has melted and the chops are done.

Serves 4.

Lamb Chops Parmesan

6 loin lamb chops	¼ cup tomato sauce
1 clove garlic, crushed	1 tablespoon chopped parsley
1 tablespoon olive oil	½ teaspoon dried oregano
3 tablespoons grated Parmesan cheese	freshly ground black pepper

1. Secure the tails of the chops with a toothpick. Preheat the broiler.
2. Sauté garlic in oil in a frying pan until just brown. Stir in the cheese, tomato sauce, parsley, oregano and pepper.
3. Place a thin layer of the cheese mixture on top of each chop. Broil for 5 minutes, turn and spread the remaining mixture on the other side of the chop. Broil a further 5 minutes or until done to taste. Serve immediately.

Serves 6.

Mint Lamb Chops

6 loin lamb chops,
cut thickly
1 tablespoon lemon juice
2 tablespoons oil
2 tablespoons mint jelly

1. Secure the tails with toothpicks and rub lemon juice into each side and rub in the oil. Let stand for 1 hour. Pop the chops under a pre-heated broiler for about 1 minute to sear each side.
2. Brush the top of the chops with some mint jelly and cook for 3 minutes. Turn and brush the other side with the remaining mint jelly. Cook until done, brushing any melted mint jelly over the chops during the cooking time.

These chops are nice served with minted potatoes and glazed carrots.

Serves 6.

Savory Chops

6 leg lamb chops	½ teaspoon mustard
2 tablespoons brown sugar	1 teaspoon basil or mixed herbs
2 tablespoons flour	salt and pepper
2 tablespoons lemon juice	1½ cups (375 ml) water
2 tablespoons tomato sauce	2 tablespoons sherry
1 teaspoon ginger	½ cup sour cream
1 teaspoon curry powder	

1. Trim the fat from the chops and place in a casserole.
2. Mix the rest of the ingredients except the sour cream and pour over the chops and leave to marinate at room temperature for at least 3 hours.
3. Cover the dish and bake for 2 hours in a slow oven 300°F (150°C).
4. Just before serving pour in the sour cream. If the sauce is too thin add a little cornstarch and water.

Serves 6.

Oriental Lamb

1½ lb (750 g) leg chops	salt and pepper
1 tablespoon oil	1 teaspoon ground ginger
1 cup diced pineapple	1 cup (250 ml) pineapple juice
1 onion, chopped	1 teaspoon soya sauce
3 slices bacon	½ cup (125 ml) water
1 tablespoon flour	1 dessertspoon chopped mint

1. Cut the lamb into 1 inch (2½ cm) cubes and brown in hot oil. Remove the meat and add pineapple and brown lightly, remove the pineapple and add chopped bacon, onions and cook until brown.
2. Stir in the flour, salt and pepper, ginger, pineapple juice, soya sauce, and water. When boiling add the meat and cook for at least 1 hour. Add the pineapple and cook a further 30 minutes.
3. Serve immediately sprinkled with parsley.

Serves 4.

Spicy Lamb Shoulder Chops

4 lamb shoulder chops
1 small onion, sliced
1 green pepper, sliced
1 tablespoon brown sugar
8 oz (250 g) tomato purée

½ teaspoon dry mustard
½ teaspoon basil
½ teaspoon salt
1 teaspoon horseradish sauce
2 tablespoons vinegar

1. Place the meat in a casserole dish.
2. Arrange the sliced onions and green peppers on top of the chops.
3. Mix the remaining ingredients together and pour the mixture over the meat. Cover the casserole and cook in a moderate oven 350°F (180°C) for about 1 hour.

Serves 4.

Lamb Kebabs — Greek Style

2 lb (1 kg) boned lamb, from
  the leg or shoulder
small tomatoes
  (or larger ones, cubed)
zucchini, par-boiled for
  2 minutes
1 red pepper
1 green pepper
small mushroom caps

¼ cup olive oil
4 tablespoons lemon juice
½ cup (125 ml) white wine
1 teaspoon salt
freshly ground black pepper
½ teaspoon marjoram
3 cloves garlic, crushed
3 bay leaves, crushed

1. Mix all the ingredients apart from the lamb and vegetables and pour over the lamb in a bowl and marinate for at least 8 hours. Turn occasionally.
2. Place the pieces of lamb with a piece of bay leaf between each piece on a skewer. On separate skewers alternate pieces of the vegetables.
3. Preheat the broiler until very hot and cook brushing the meat and vegetables with the marinade and turning the skewers once or twice.

Serves 6-8.

Lamb Teriyaki

1½ lb (750 g) lamb from shoulder or leg, boned and cubed	1 tablespoon white wine vinegar
2 medium white onions	2 tablespoons honey
1 green pepper	1 cup dry sherry
1 red pepper	1 cup water
¼ cup soya sauce	1 teaspoon ground ginger

1. Quarter the onions and cut the peppers into 1 inch (2½ cm) squares. Thread the lamb, onions and peppers alternatively onto skewers and marinate in a mixture of the rest of the ingredients which has been boiled and simmered for 2 minutes. Marinate for at least 3 hours, turning regularly.
2. Broil under a hot broiler until the meat is crisp and brown on all sides, baste while cooking with the remaining marinade.
3. Thicken the rest of the marinade in a small saucepan with a little cornstarch.

Serves 4.

Shish Kebabs

2 lb (1 kg) leg lamb, 1 inch (2½ cm) cubes	2 zucchini, sliced
1 cup buttermilk (skim milk or yoghurt will do)	2 tablespoons oil
freshly ground black pepper	salt
thyme	1 green pepper, cut into squares
8 large mushroom caps	12 cherry tomatoes (chopped large tomatoes)
	8 small onions

1. Mix buttermilk, pepper and thyme in a large bowl and marinate the meat for at least 2 hours at room temperature, turning a number of times.
2. Place the oil and salt in another bowl and marinate the mushroom caps and sliced zucchini turning so that they are well coated with the seasoned oil.
3. Drain the meat and alternatively place the meat and vegetables on skewers. Broil under a hot preheated broiler until the meat is well browned and sizzling.

Serves 4-6.

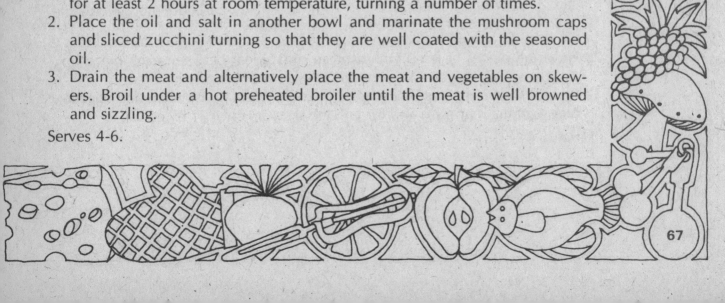

Lamb with Vermouth

1 leg lamb
2 cloves garlic
1 teaspoon rosemary
2 tablespoons olive oil
salt and pepper
1½ cups (375 ml) dry vermouth

1. Wipe the lamb with oil and salt and pepper and make small incisions over the surface and put in small pieces of garlic and some rosemary spikes.
2. Roast in a moderate oven 350°F (180°C) for 45 minutes. Warm 1 cup of the vermouth and pour over the lamb and return to oven and cook basting and turning the lamb for the remainder of the cooking time calculated at 30 minutes per pound (1 hour per kg). If using a thermometer, it should read 175°F (80°C).
3. Remove the fat from the baking dish and add ½ cup dry vermouth, bring to boil and adjust the seasoning. Thicken with a little cornstarch if desired.

Serves 6-8.

Shaslik Russian Style

1½ lb (750 g) boned loin, leg, shoulder of lamb, hogget or mutton
8 oz (250 g) bacon slices
6 small tomatoes
½ cup (125 ml) vodka

4 tablespoons oil
2 tablespoons lemon juice
1 bay leaf, crushed
pinch thyme, rosemary, cumin
salt and pepper

1. Cut the meat into 1 inch (2½ cm) cubes and place in a dish, add the salt and pepper and herbs and cover with the vodka, oil and lemon juice.
2. Marinate the meat for 4 hours, turning regularly.
3. Cut the slices into three pieces and roll up.
4. Place the meat and bacon alternatively onto skewers and finish with a tomato at the end.
5. Broil under a preheated hot broiler for 12 minutes basting with the marinade two or three times.

Serves 4-6.

Baked Lamb Breasts with Apples and Apricots

.4 breasts of lamb
2 large onions, chopped
1 tablespoon (20 g) butter
2 teaspoons curry powder
1 large cooking apple, peeled and chopped
½ cup dried apricots

2 tablespoons brown sugar
1 tablespoon coconut
½ teaspoon nutmeg and cinnamon mixed
1½ cups (375 ml) water
1 teaspoon salt
¼ cup raisins

1. Buy the breasts of lamb with the bones still in. Cut between the bones into strips (2 bones to each strip). Place the strips in a baking dish and bake in a hot oven 425°F (200°C) for 30 minutes. Turn the pieces once or twice.
2. Meanwhile sauté the onion in butter until soft and add curry powder, apple, apricots, brown sugar, coconut, nutmeg, cinnamon and water. Stir and cover and simmer gently for 30 minutes.
3. Drain the fat from the lamb and reduce the oven to 325°F (160°C). Pour the fruit sauce through and over the lamb and season with salt and pepper and sprinkle with the raisins. Cover the dish with foil and cook for a further 45 minutes. Take the foil off the pan for the last 10 minutes. Skim off excess fat and serve with hot rice.

Serves 4.

Barbecued Leg of Lamb

large leg of lamb
flour
salt and pepper
1 onion, sliced

1 cup (250 ml) water
½ cup (125 ml) tomato sauce
2 tablespoons Worcestershire sauce

1. Place the lamb in a baking dish and surround with the sliced onions. Combine all the other ingredients and sauces and pour over the meat.
2. Roast in a moderate 350°F (180°C) oven for 30 minutes to each pound (60 minutes per kg). Baste frequently.
3. Pour off any excess fat and make a gravy with the basting sauce.

Serves 6-8.

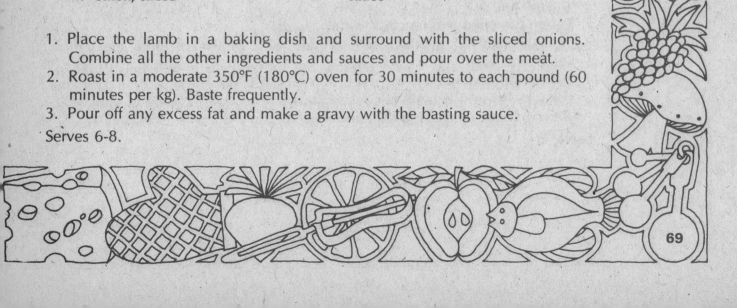

Coffee—Basted Lamb

1 leg lamb
salt and pepper
1 cup (250 ml) strong coffee (or double strength instant)
½ cup cream

1 teaspoon sugar
water
2 tablespoons flour
2 tablespoons red currant jelly

1. Rub salt and pepper over the surface of the lamb and bake in a moderate oven 350°F (180°C) for 1 hour.
2. Mix the coffee, cream and sugar and pour over the lamb. Continue cooking for the remainder of the cooking time, calculated at 30 minutes per pound (60 minutes per 1 kg) basting frequently. Add a little water if the liquid evaporates too much during cooking.
3. When cooked remove the lamb, skim off fat from the pan, putting aside 2 tablespoons of fat in a saucepan. Add enough water to the roasting pan to make 2 cups of liquid, stir well lifting off any baked on juices.
4. Heat the fat in the saucepan, stir in the flour and cook for one minute. Add the liquid from the roasting pan and stir until the sauce thickens and boils. Add the red currant jelly and stir until the jelly is completely absorbed.

Baked Stuffed Leg of Lamb

1 leg lamb, boned
1 cup soft breadcrumbs
½ teaspoon celery salt
½ teaspoon salt
black pepper
1 small can of crushed pineapple, drained

2 cloves garlic, crushed
1 tablespoon (20 g) butter
½ teaspoon ground ginger
2 tablespoons lemon juice
red currant jelly

1. Rub the lamb both inside and out with salt and pepper. Mix breadcrumbs, celery salt, salt and pepper, garlic and pineapple and stuff the lamb with the mixture.
2. Fasten the open end together with skewers.
3. Rub the lamb with butter and sprinkle with ginger and pour the lemon juice over it.
4. Bake in a moderately slow oven 325°F (160°C) for about 2 hours. Fifteen minutes before the lamb is cooked glaze the top with the red currant jelly. Remove from the baking dish and make a gravy from the drippings.

Serves 6-8.

Crown Roast of Lamb

1 crown roast
   or 2 racks of cutlets
salt and pepper
thyme and rosemary
2 cloves garlic
oil
mashed potato and grated
   cheese

1. Have the butcher prepare the crown roast allowing 2 cutlets per person.
2. Rub salt and pepper inside and out of the roast, sprinkle lightly with thyme and rosemary and rub over with the garlic. Brush the outside with oil. Insert a wad of aluminum foil in the center of the crown so that roast retains its shape during cooking. Also cover the tips of bone with some foil to stop them burning. Place in a baking dish and cook at 350°F (180°C) for 1 hour.
3. Remove the foil from the center of the roast, fill with mashed potato and sprinkle with grated cheese. Return to the oven and cook until the cheese and potato are brown, about 15 minutes. Remove the foil from the tips and if you wish add cutlet frills.
4. Make a gravy from the baking dish and serve with vegetables around the roast.

Serves 4-6.

Fried Liver

1½ lb (750 g) liver
3 tablespoons lemon juice
½ cup (60 g) flour
1 teaspoon basil
salt and pepper
½ cup cream

1 grated onion
2 beaten eggs
2 cloves garlic
2 cups dry cracker crumbs
½ cup (125 g) butter

1. Remove the membrane from the liver, slice and sprinkle with lemon juice.
2. Combine all the dry ingredients and roll the liver in the mixture.
3. Mix cream, onion, eggs and garlic together and dip the liver in this mixture and then dip again into the cracker crumbs.
4. Fry quickly on both sides in hot butter.

Serves 4.

Lamb Eastern Style

1 shoulder of lamb, boned (a leg may also be used)
2 small onions, chopped
1 tablespoon (20 g) butter
½ teaspoon curry powder
1 tablespoon currants
1 tablespoon raisins
1 cup cooked rice

1 teaspoon grated lemon rind
1 tablespoon lemon juice
1 egg yolk, beaten
salt and pepper
1 tablespoon mango chutney (optional)
1 tablespoon flour
1¼ cups (300 ml) dry white wine

1. Sauté the onion in butter until soft. Add the curry, currants, raisins and rice. Mix over the heat and add the lemon rind, salt and pepper to taste.
2. Open out the shoulder (or make a pocket in the leg) to hold the stuffing. Spread the stuffing over the lamb and roll up, secure with skewers or string. Rub the surfaces with salt and pepper and bake in a moderate oven 350°F (180°C) for 1½ hours. Turn occasionally to brown all surfaces.
3. Remove the lamb to a plate and keep warm for 15 minutes before carving.
4. Drain off the excess fat from the baking dish leaving about 1 tablespoon of fat. Stir in the flour and cook gently on top of the stove for 1 minute. Stir in the wine and cook until smooth. Add chutney and lemon juice, season to taste.

Serves 4-6.

Lamb and Apricot Stew

½ cup dried apricots
2½ lb (1¼ kg) breast of lamb
1 onion, chopped
1 tablespoon brown sugar

1 teaspoon soya sauce
1 tablespoon dry sherry
salt and pepper

1. Soak the apricots. Cut the meat into 1 inch (2½ cm) cubes and place in a saucepan and cover with boiling water, add the onion and simmer for 1 hour.
2. Remove the meat and place in a casserole. Cool the stock from the lamb and remove the fat.
3. Add the apricots, brown sugar, soya sauce, dry sherry, salt and pepper and cover with the stock. Bake for 1 hour.
4. Thicken the sauce if necessary and return to oven and bake uncovered for another ¼ hour.

Serves 4-6.

Orange Lamb

    1 leg lamb (or other
       baking joint)
    rind of 1 orange, grated
    salt and pepper
    1 cup (250 ml) orange juice
    1 tablespoon brown sugar
    1 teaspoon dry mustard

1. Rub the lamb all over with salt and pepper and rub the orange rind well in.
2. Cook in a moderate oven 350°F (180°C) for 40 minutes.
3. Mix orange juice, brown sugar and mustard together and pour over the lamb. Return the lamb to the oven and cook the lamb the remainder of cooking time, calculated at 30 minutes per pound (60 minutes per 1 kg). Baste frequently with the pan juices. Add some water or more orange juice to the pan if it becomes too dry.
4. When cooked place on a dish and keep warm for 15 minutes before carving.
5. Skim the fat from the pan drippings and add some stock or water and stir over heat on the top of the stove. Bring to the boil, season to taste. The gravy may be thickened with a little cornstarch if desired.

Roasted sweet potatoes are delicious with this lamb.

Serves 6-8.

Kidney Pudding

    4 sheep kidneys
    1 cup breadcrumbs
    1 cup minced suet
    salt and pepper
    ½ teaspoon nutmeg
    1 egg
    1 cup (250 ml) milk

1. Remove the membrane and fat from the kidneys and cut into small pieces and mix with dry ingredients.
2. Mix the egg and milk together and then mix with the kidneys.
3. Pour into a buttered mold and steam for 1 hour.

Serve with a rich gravy.

Serves 4.

Lamb Navarin

2 lb (1 kg) boneless lamb (from shoulder)	½ teaspoon brown sugar
	salt and pepper
2 tablespoons (40 g) butter	mixed herbs
1 onion, chopped	8 small white whole onions
2 cloves garlic, crushed	1 turnip, sliced
2 tablespoons flour	12 small whole potatoes
2 tablespoons tomato paste	1 cup fresh shelled peas
1 cup (250 ml) stock (use a beef cube)	

1. Brown the meat in the butter in a pan. Transfer the meat to a casserole dish. Sauté the onion and garlic in the same pan and stir in the flour and cook until lightly colored. Add stock stirring until smooth and thick. Add the tomato paste, sugar, salt and pepper and pour over the lamb. Sprinkle over some mixed herbs. Cover and cook in a slow oven 325°F (160°C) for 1 hour.
2. Add the whole onions, turnip, potatoes and peas and cover and cook for another hour or until meat is tender and vegetables are cooked.

Serves 4-6.

Lamb a la Nicoise

1 loin or shoulder of lamb, boned and rolled	1 small eggplant
	1 large tomato, skinned
2 tablespoons olive oil	1½ lb (750 g) small new potatoes
salt and pepper	
1 onion, sliced	chopped parsley
8 oz (250 g) zucchini	

1. Rub 1 tablespoon olive oil over the lamb and sprinkle with salt and pepper. Bake in a moderate oven 350°F (180°C) for 45 minutes.
2. Sauté the onion in the remaining oil until soft.
3. Cut the zucchini and unpeeled eggplant into ½ inch (1 cm) cubes, sprinkle with salt and allow to stand 20 minutes. Drain and dry and mix with the cooked onion, chopped tomato and potatoes and place vegetables around the lamb. Season with a little salt and pepper and return to the oven. Reduce the heat of the oven to 325°F (160°C) and cook for a further 45 minutes, add some white wine or stock during the cooking if the mixture becomes dry. Serve the lamb sliced thickly surrounding it with the vegetables. Sprinkle with chopped parsley.

Serves 4-6.

Lamb Stuffed with Rice

3 oz (90 g) rice
juice of 1 lemon
1 onion chopped
1 tablespoon oil
2 cloves garlic
3 oz (90 g) seedless raisins
salt and pepper

1 boned shoulder lamb
2 tablespoons oil or butter
1 tablespoon flour
1 tablespoon tomato juice
   or purée
¼ pint (150 ml) water
½ lb (250 g) tomatoes, sliced

1. Wash rice and cook in fast boiling water with lemon juice for 15 minutes, drain and dry.
2. Brown the onion in some oil or melted butter, stir in the garlic and raisins. Put in a bowl and mix with the rice. Season to taste.
3. Stuff the meat and secure with string. Place in a baking dish and pour over oil and sprinkle with salt and pepper and roast for 1½ hours at 400°F (200°C). Reduce the heat to 325°F (160°C) and cook for 50 minutes or until done.
4. Take the lamb from the baking dish and pour off excess fat. Make a sauce by adding the flour and stirring until smooth. Add the tomato juice or purée and blend with the water. Stir until sauce thickens. Pour over the meat and garnish with tomato slices.

Serves 4.

Spicy Lamb Shanks

6 lamb shanks
flour
salt and pepper
1 cup (250 ml) white wine
1 cup cooked prunes, seeded
1 cup cooked dried apricots
½ cup brown sugar

1 tablespoon honey
½ teaspoon cinnamon
½ teaspoon ginger
¼ teaspoon cloves
3 tablespoons lemon juice
salt and pepper

1. Roll the shanks in seasoned flour and place in a greased casserole dish. Cover and bake at 350°F (180°C) for 1 hour. Remove from the oven. Pour over a little oil.
2. Meanwhile mix all the other ingredients in a saucepan and simmer for 7 minutes.
3. Pour the fruit mixture over the meat, cover and bake at 375°F (190°C) for a further 1½ hours or until done.

Serves 6.

Sweet and Sour Lamb

1 lb (500 g) lean lamb from
the leg
4 tablespoons peanut oil
1 large onion, sliced
1 green pepper, cut into strips
1 carrot, sliced
2 cloves garlic, crushed
½ teaspoon ground ginger
1 can 14 oz (425 g) pineapple
pieces

juice from the pineapple pieces
2 tablespoons cornstarch
3 tablespoons lemon juice
2 tablespoons dry sherry
2 teaspoons soya sauce
2 teaspoons brown sugar
salt and pepper
2 oz (60 g) chow mein noodles,
boiled and drained
oil for frying noodles

1. Cut the lamb into thin strips and brown quickly in 2 tablespoons hot oil. Remove the lamb and set aside.
2. Add the remaining oil to the frypan and sauté onion, green pepper, carrot, garlic and ginger for 4 minutes stirring regularly. Remove from the heat.
3. Drain the pineapple and reserve the juice. Measure the juice and if it does not make 1½ cups (375 ml) add some water. Add this to the pan with the pineapple pieces.
4. Blend the cornstarch with the sherry, soya sauce, lemon juice, sugar and salt and pepper. Return to the heat and stir until the mixture thickens. Return the lamb to the pan and cover and simmer gently for 15 minutes. Do not boil.

Serve with the crisp fried noodles and/or boiled rice.

Serves 6.

Roasted Lamb Shanks

6 lamb shanks
6 cloves garlic
1 teaspoon thyme or rosemary
salt and pepper

4 tablespoons flour
2 tablespoons oil
1 chicken stock cube
1 cup (250 ml) water

1. Insert into each shank a clove of garlic by making a small slit in each. Roll the shanks in seasoned flour and brown in some oil; in a baking dish.
2. Remove the meat from the pan and add flour and blend well with the oil. Slowly pour in 1 cup of water in which the chicken cube has been dissolved and cook until thickened, stirring all the time. Season.
3. Add the shanks to the sauce and bake in a moderate oven 350°F (180°C) for about 1½ hours turning the shanks all the time. More liquid may be added to the sauce if required. Remove the garlic and serve immediately.

Serves 6.

Moussaka

2 brown onions, finely chopped
3 cloves garlic, crushed
6 tablespoons olive oil
2 lbs (1 kg) cooked ground lamb
6 tomatoes, skinned and chopped
1 lb (500 g) mushrooms
2 tablespoons chopped parsley

salt and pepper
4 tablespoons tomato paste
½ cup meat stock
6 eggplants
flour
olive oil
Parmesan cheese, grated

1. Sauté the onions and garlic in oil. Add the ground cooked lamb and brown. Add the tomatoes, mushrooms, parsley, salt and pepper and cook until the onion is tender.
2. Mix the tomato paste and stock together and add it to the pan and simmer a further 10 minutes.
3. Slice the unpeeled eggplant lengthwise, sprinkle with salt and pepper and let drain for about 15 minutes. Remove the moisture and sprinkle with flour. Sauté both sides in hot oil. Drain.
4. Line a casserole dish with the eggplant, spread over a layer of the meat mixture and sprinkle cheese. Repeat the layers finishing with the eggplant and cheese.
5. Bake in a moderate oven 375°F (190°C) until the top is nicely brown. Serve hot or cold.

Serves 4-6.

Glazed Smoked Mutton or Lamb

1 leg of smoked mutton or lamb
½ cup brown sugar
1 teaspoon mustard

1 cup (250 ml) orange
  or pineapple juice
cloves

1. Soak the meat in cold water for 1 hour. Place in a large saucepan or boiler and cover with water, bring to the boil and simmer for 25 minutes per pound (25 minutes per 500 g).
2. Allow the leg to cool in the liquid. Mix the brown sugar, mustard and fruit juice. Score the cooked cooled leg in a criss-cross pattern and place in a baking dish. Stud the crosses with a clove and pour over the fruit mixture. Bake in a moderate oven for 40 minutes, basting regularly with the pan juices.

Serve hot or cold.

Serves 4-6.

77

Kidneys Italian Style

6 kidneys
1 level tablespoon flour
salt and pepper
3 slices bacon
½ cup (125 ml) water
1 beef cube
3 tomatoes, sliced

12 blanched almonds
2 cloves garlic, crushed
6 olives, green
1 teaspoon brown sugar
Worcestershire sauce
chopped parsley

1. Remove membrane and fat from the kidneys and roll in seasoned flour.
2. Chop the bacon and fry with the kidneys until brown. Add the beef cube dissolved in the water and simmer until the kidneys are tender.
3. Add the tomatoes, almonds, garlic, olives, sugar and a dash of Worcestershire sauce. Thicken with cornstarch if necessary. Serve immediately. Sprinkle with parsley.

Serves 4-6.

Kidneys in Sherry

12 sheeps kidneys
1 large onion, chopped
1 tablespoon oil
1 tablespoon (20 g) butter

salt and pepper
½ cup (125 ml) sherry
1 tablespoon water
chopped parsley

1. Remove the skin from the kidneys, halve and cut out any core.
2. Sauté onion in the oil and butter until soft and golden. Lift out and set aside.
3. Brown the kidneys quickly on each side. Return the onion to the pan and add seasoning, sherry and stock; bring almost to the boil and reduce to simmer for 15 minutes, covered.
4. Thicken the sauce with a little cornstarch mixed in water. Serve.

Serves 4-6.

Brains in a Cream Sauce

6 sets lamb's brains
2 small onions, sliced
1 carrot, sliced
1 small stalk celery
1 bay leaf
salt and pepper

3 tablespoons (60 g) butter
3 tablespoons flour
¾ cup (187.5 ml) milk
4 oz (125 g) mushrooms sauteed
  in butter with lemon juice
  from 1 lemon

1. Soak brains in cold water for ½ hour. Remove any loose skin and put in a saucepan with the onion, carrot, celery and bay leaf. Add enough water to just cover the brains and bring to a simmer. Cover and simmer for 5 minutes, add salt and pepper and cook again for 10 minutes.
2. Drain the liquid from the brains, measure and set aside ½ cup of the stock. Discard the bay leaf but retain the vegetables.
3. Cut the brains into small pieces. Melt the butter in a saucepan, stir in the flour. Cook for 1 minute and stir in the milk slowly and the reserved stock, stirring all the time and cook until sauce thickens and boils. Season with lemon juice.
4. Gently stir in the brains and vegetables and season to taste.

Serves 4-6.

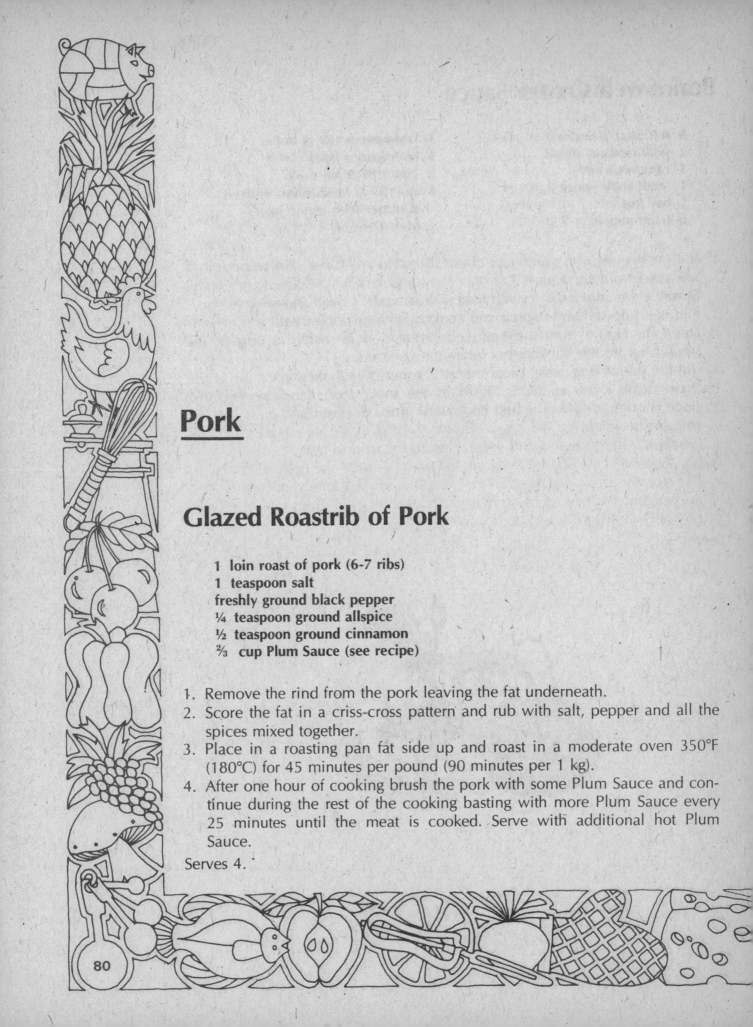

Pork

Glazed Roastrib of Pork

1 loin roast of pork (6-7 ribs)
1 teaspoon salt
freshly ground black pepper
¼ teaspoon ground allspice
½ teaspoon ground cinnamon
⅔ cup Plum Sauce (see recipe)

1. Remove the rind from the pork leaving the fat underneath.
2. Score the fat in a criss-cross pattern and rub with salt, pepper and all the spices mixed together.
3. Place in a roasting pan fat side up and roast in a moderate oven 350°F (180°C) for 45 minutes per pound (90 minutes per 1 kg).
4. After one hour of cooking brush the pork with some Plum Sauce and continue during the rest of the cooking basting with more Plum Sauce every 25 minutes until the meat is cooked. Serve with additional hot Plum Sauce.

Serves 4.

Pork Swedish Style

4 lb (2 kg) boned loin of pork with rind removed	salt and pepper
10 prunes, stoned	3 tablespoons (60 g) butter
1 large apple, peeled, cored and cut into 1 inch cubes	3 tablespoons oil
2 teaspoons lemon juice	1½ cups (375 ml) white wine
	¾ cup cream
	2 tablespoons red currant jelly

1. Put the prunes in a saucepan, cover with water and boil. Set aside for 30 minutes and then drain.
2. Sprinkle the cubed apple with lemon juice and mix with prunes.
3. Cut a slit down the length of the loin or make a pocket with a skewer in the loin. Season with salt and pepper and stuff with the prunes and apples. Fasten the slit together.
4. Tie the loin at 1½ inch (4 cm) intervals so as to keep its shape.
5. Preheat the oven at 350°F (180°C). Melt the butter in a casserole dish large enough for the pork and brown the pork on all sides.
6. Remove the fat from the casserole and pour over the wine and stir in the cream.
7. Cook in the center of the oven for 1½ hours or until the pork is tender.
8. Remove the pork and keep warm. On top of the stove reduce the wine and cream sauce in the casserole dish to about 1 cup, mix in the red currant jelly and stir until smooth. Serve.

Serves 6.

Roast Loin of Pork with Stuffed Apples

1 loin of pork, boned and rolled
Stuffed Apples:
6 red apples
1 cup soft breadcrumbs
8 prunes, seeded and chopped
2 tablespoons chopped walnuts
grated rind of 1 lemon

1 teaspoon brown sugar
½ teaspoon cinnamon
2 tablespoons (40 g) melted butter
salt to taste
1 egg, beaten

1. Preheat the oven at 450°F (230°C). Rub the scoured rind of the pork with salt and place on a rack in a baking dish and cook for 30 minutes until crackling is crisp and brown. Do not baste crackling during any part of the cooking.
2. Reduce the oven to 350°F (180°C) and complete the cooking allowing 45 minutes per pound (90 minutes per 1 kg).
3. Mix the ingredients for the stuffing of the apples together and fill the cored red apples whose skin has been removed from the top. Some apple may be scooped out to allow for more stuffing. Brush the top of apples with some melted butter, place on a square of aluminum foil and bring the foil up around the apples to form a small cup. Cook on the rack around the pork, about 1 hour before the end of the cooking.

Serves 6.

Cheese Coated Pork Chops

6 pork loin or rib chops
salt and pepper
½ cup of Swiss cheese
2 tablespoons cream
½ teaspoon dry mustard

1. Broil the chops under a moderate heat until browned and thoroughly cooked. Season with salt and pepper.
2. Take the chops from the broiler and spread a mixture of the cheese and cream over the chops. Return to the hot broiler and broil until golden brown. Serve immediately.

Serves 4-6.

Roast Pork Oriental Style

1 shoulder of pork, boned
1½ teaspoons salt
½ cup soya sauce
⅓ cup lemon juice
½ cup (60 g) white sugar

½ teaspoon red food coloring
1 small onion, chopped
¾ teaspoon ground ginger
2 cloves garlic

1. Remove the rind from the pork but leave the fat on underneath.
2. Mix all the ingredients together in a basin and place the pork fat side up, in the marinade and refrigerate for 8 hours or overnight.
3. Remove and roll the pork up securing with skewers or string. Place on a rack in a baking dish and cook in a moderate oven 375°F (180°C) for 45 minutes per pound (90 minutes per 1 kg).
4. Baste regularly during the cooking with the marinade. When the pork is cooked remove and make a gravy by thickening the remaining marinade with a little cornstarch.

Serves 4.

Pork Chops (Shoulder)

6 pork chops	1 cup crushed pineapple
1 teaspoon ground ginger	3 tablespoons (60 ml) white wine
1 teaspoon paprika	2 tablespoons honey
salt and pepper	2 tablespoons soya sauce
¼ cup flour	

1. Mix ginger, salt, pepper, paprika and flour. Roll the chops thoroughly and brown them in some hot bacon fat.
2. Mix the rest of the ingredients together and pour over the chops. Cover and cook slowly until tender.
3. Thicken the gravy with a little cornstarch and serve with fluffy rice.

Serves 4-6.

Spanish Pork Chops

4 pork chops, loin	salt and freshly ground
1 tablespoon olive oil	black pepper
1 onion, sliced	pinch rosemary
2 cloved garlic, crushed	2 tablespoons port
1 cup chopped, peeled tomatoes	

1. Cook the chops in oil in a frying pan until browned and cooked through. Remove and keep warm.
2. Drain except for 1 tablespoon of fat. Fry the onion and garlic, stirring to lift pan juices, add the tomatoes, salt and pepper to taste. Add the rosemary and port and simmer for 5 minutes. Pour the sauce over the chops and serve immediately.

Serves 4.

Pork Chops with Prunes

6 pork chops, loin, rib or leg	2 whole cloves
2 tablespoons oil or butter	½ teaspoon cinnamon
1 cup prunes, seeded	salt and pepper
½ cup sweet vermouth	1 teaspoon lemon juice
¼ cup (63 ml) water	

1. In a small saucepan combine the prunes, vermouth, water, cloves and cinnamon. Bring to the boil and remove and allow to stand while the chops are cooking. Remove cloves just before serving.
2. Heat the oil or butter in a pan and brown the chops on each side. Reduce the heat and complete the cooking turning occasionally. Remove and keep warm.
3. Drain off most of the fat from the pan and add spiced prune mixture, bring to the boil and add lemon juice and boil until slightly reduced. Thicken with a little cornstarch, season to taste and pour over the chops. Serve immediately.

Serves 4-6.

Pork with Honey

2 lb (1 kg) pork, chopped to 1 inch (2½ cm) cubes	¾ cup yoghurt
1½ tablespoons honey	grated peel of an orange
60 g (2 oz) butter	grated peel of a lemon
2 grated onions	2 cloves garlic, crushed
½ teaspoon turmeric	4 ground cardamon seeds
½ teaspoon ground black pepper	½ teaspoon cinnamon
	¼ teaspoon ground mace

1. Heat a large saucepan and pour in the honey, stir until it sticks but is not caramelized. Add the butter and when hot add the pork cubes. Stir until brown for about 10 minutes.
2. Add 1 cup (250 ml) of water, season with salt, boil then simmer gently until pork is tender.
3. Meanwhile, mix the grated onions, turmeric, pepper, orange and lemon peel, garlic, cardamon, cinnamon and mace.
4. When the pork is done boil rapidly until all the mixture has gone, add the mixed seasonings and toss. Cook again until the butter separates. Add half the yoghurt and cook again until the butter again separates. Add the rest of the yoghurt and heat for about 5 minutes. Serve over a bed of rice.

Serves 4-6.

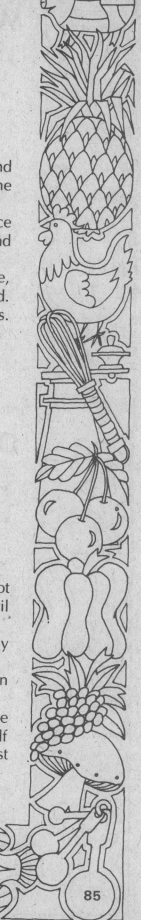

Marinated Tenderloin of Pork

1 lb (500 g) pork tenderloin
2 tablespoons soya sauce
1 tablespoon brandy
1 tablespoon brown sugar

2 cloves of garlic, crushed
1 teaspoon ginger
salt and pepper
2 tablespoons tomato sauce

1. Mix all the ingredients together and pour over pork tenderloin and marinate for at least 1 hour at room temperature.
2. Broil slowly turning frequently and basting with marinade until brown and crispy.

Serves 4.

Orange Pork Chops

6 pork rib chops
grated rind of 1 orange
salt and pepper
2 teaspoons flour
½ cup (125 ml) orange juice

1 tablespoon dry sherry
2 teaspoons brown sugar
slivers of orange peel, blanched
parsley

1. Rub the grated orange rind into the chops and allow to stand for 15 minutes.
2. Grease and heat a frying pan and cook the chops over a moderate heat until well cooked. When cooked place aside and season with salt and pepper.
3. Drain off all but 2 teaspoons fat from the pan and stir in the flour and cook for a minute. Remove from the heat and stir in the orange juice, sherry and sugar. Return to heat and stir until the sauce is thick. Pour the sauce over the chops and sprinkle with slivers of orange peel and a sprinkle of parsley.

Serves 4-6.

Pork and Apple Pie

2 lb (1 kg) pork pieces	1 lb (500 g) well drained,
1 large onion, chopped	cooked apples
salt and pepper	¾ lb (375 g) short pastry,
stock made from chicken cubes	fresh or frozen

1. Place pork, onion, salt and pepper in a saucepan and half cover with stock. Cook slowly for at least 1 hour.
2. Remove the meat from the stock and cool.
3. Line a pie dish with some pastry and cover with cold cooked apples, add the cold pork and add some more apples on top of the pork, season and cover with more pastry.
4. Bake in an oven at 400°F (200°C) for about 30 minutes or until the pastry is nicely brown.

This pie may be served hot or cold.

Serves 6.

Shepherds Pork Pie

4 lb (2 kg) lean pork	1 teaspoon cinnamon
1 inch (2½ cm) cubes	salt and pepper
5 apples, peeled, cored and sliced	1 beef cube and water for stock
2 onions, sliced	mashed potatoes
1 teaspoon sage	

1. Put layers of chopped pork and sliced apples in layers in a deep baking dish.
2. Sprinkle each layer with sliced onions, sage, cinnamon and salt and pepper.
3. Pour over a little stock (just to moisten only).
4. Cover the top with mashed potatoes and brush with a little melted butter.
5. Bake in a slow oven 325°F (160°C) for 2 hours.

Serves 8.

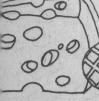

Meat Ring

1½ lb (750 g) finely ground beef	½ cup crackers, crushed
1 lb (500 g) finely ground pork	salt and pepper
1 onion, grated	⅓ cup evaporated milk
1 teaspoon prepared mustard	
2 beaten eggs	

1. Blend all the ingredients thoroughly together press into a greased ring cake pan and bake in a moderate oven 350°F (180°C) for 1½ hours.
2. Unmold onto a serving plate and fill center with vegetables e.g. a mixture of peas and corn, broccoli or cauliflower.

Serve with mashed or boiled potatoes.

Serve 6-8.

Sausages Jambalaya

1 lb (500 g) thick pork sausages	1 teaspoon brown sugar
2 slices bacon, chopped	dash Tabasco sauce
1 onion, chopped	2 cups (500 ml) white wine
1 tablespoon (20 g) butter	1½ cups rice
1 can chopped tomatoes, skinned	chopped parsley
1 tablespoon tomato sauce	salt and pepper

1. Place the sausages in a saucepan of hot water, bring to a slow simmer and cook very gently for 10 minutes. Do not boil or the skins will burst. Drain and cut into thick slices.
2. In a greased frying pan (with a lid) brown the sausage slices and lift out. Drain off fat from the pan and cook the bacon until crisp, add the onion and butter and saute over a low heat until the onion is golden. Add the tomatoes, tomato and Tabasco sauce, wine, sugar and salt and pepper. Bring to boil, stir in the rice and sausage slices and return again to the boil.
3. Reduce the heat, cover and cook, stirring occasionally, until the rice is cooked (about 25 minutes). Sprinkle with chopped parsley.

Serve with a tossed salad on the side.

Serves 4-5.

Spareribs of Beef or Pork

4-6 lb (2 kg - 3 kg) pork ribs
   or beef ribs
½ cup oil
1 tablespoon grated onion
2 cloves garlic

1 cup apple sauce
4 tablespoons lemon juice
1 teaspoon ground ginger
salt and pepper

1. Place the spareribs in a bowl and mix the remaining ingredients together and pour over the spareribs. Stir well and leave at room temperature for several hours. Turning regularly.
2. Broil under a moderate temperature turning and basting frequently with the marinade for about ¾ hour, or until the pork or beef is tender.
3. Heat any remaining marinade and serve with the spareribs.

Serves 6-8.

Pork Satay

1 lb (500 g) pork tenderloin
½ teaspoon salt
freshly ground black pepper
1 tablespoon ground almonds

½ teaspoon ground ginger
1 teaspoon turmeric
2 teaspoons brown sugar
1 cup Coconut Milk

1. Cut the meat into bite-sized cubes. Season with salt and pepper.
2. Mix the ground almonds, ginger, turmeric, and sugar in a basin, add Coconut Milk and blend well. Add the pork pieces and stir well and marinate for at least 2 hours at room temperature.
3. Remove the pork pieces and thread onto skewers. Cook under a preheated broiler turning and basting often with the Coconut Milk mixture.

Serve immediately with rice. The remaining Coconut Milk mixture may be heated and served with the Satay.

Serves 4.

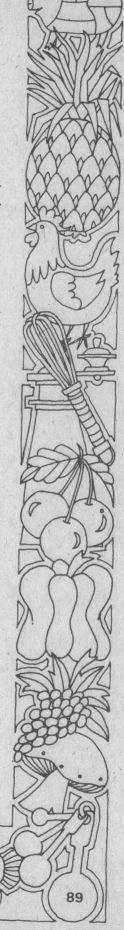

Pork Tenderloin

pork tenderloin   butter
prunes, seeded   water
finely chopped apple   flour

1. Make a slit down the center of each tenderloin and fill with prunes and finely chopped apple.
2. Fasten the edges together with a skewer.
3. Brown in some butter and add water to the pan and simmer gently for 1 hour.

Pork Chop Roll

6 pork chops
1 cup chopped celery
1 cup chopped onion
3 tablespoons (60 g) butter
3 cups cubed day-old bread
salt and pepper
3 tablespoons parsley

1. Brown the pork chops in a little butter in a frying pan.
2. Add the onion and celery and cook until golden brown. Mix in the bread cubes, salt, pepper and parsley.
3. At the end of a loaf pan, place a pork chop fat side up. Alternate stuffing and chops, ending with a pork chop.
4. Bake in a slow oven 250°F (120°C) for 2 hours.

This is nice garnished with slices of pineapple or apples and parsley.

Serves 4-6.

Ham Ring

1 tablespoon (15 g) unflavored gelatin	juice of 1 lemon
¼ cup (63 ml) water	¼ teaspoon salt and pepper
¾ cup (188 ml) boiling water	1½ cups diced cooked or canned ham
1 cup (250 ml) sour cream	1 cup celery, chopped
½ cup mayonnaise or salad dressing	2 tablespoons parsley
3 tablespoons vinegar	3 tablespoons onion, grated

1. Soften the gelatin in cold water and add to the boiling water and dissolve.
2. Add gelatin to a mixture of cream, mayonnaise, vinegar, lemon juice and salt and pepper. Chill until nearly set then whip until fluffy. Fold in the remaining ingredients.
3. Pour into a ring mold and chill until firm.
4. Unmold, and fill the center with a green salad or green grapes.

Serves 4-6.

Apricot Glazed Ham

    4 lb (2 kg) cooked ham
    2 cups (500 ml) apricot nectar
    1 cup (250 ml) apple sauce
    2 tablespoons Worcestershire sauce
    ½ teaspoon dry mustard
    whole cloves
    dash of Tabasco sauce

1. Sauté the ham in a large saucepan in a little butter for about 15 minutes or until the ham is golden brown all over.
2. Score the top and sides in a criss-cross pattern.
3. Return the ham to the saucepan and cook slowly for 15 minutes making sure the ham does not stick to the pan.
4. Mix the rest of the ingredients together and pour carefully over the ham. Cover and simmer slowly for 2 hours, basting all the time.
5. Stud each cross with cloves and serve.

Serves 6-8.

Ham and Corn Pie

1 cup ground ham (or any left over cold meat)	1½ cups (375 ml) milk
1 tablespoon (20 g) butter	½ cup crispy cooked bacon, chopped
2 tablespoons flour	2 teaspoons grated onion
½ teaspoon pepper	1 tablespoon chopped parsley
1 teaspoon salt	1 small can of cream style corn
1 teaspoon brown sugar	2 eggs, lightly beaten

1. Arrange the ham or cold meat on the bottom of a shallow pie dish or baking dish.
2. Melt butter in saucepan and add the flour, salt, pepper and brown sugar. Add the milk gradually and cook over heat until the mixture thickens, stirring all the time.
3. Add the onion, corn and eggs and mix well. Do not boil. Remove from the heat and turn into the pie or baking dish and put in a pan of hot water and bake in a 375°F (190°C) oven for 45 minutes or until the mixture is firm.

Serves 4-6.

Pork Tenderloin Italian Style

3 large tomatoes, peeled and
  chopped
2 large green peppers, chopped
3 large zucchinis, chopped
1 large onion, chopped
1½ lb (750 g) pork tenderloin
  or lean pork meat
1 teaspoon salt

pepper
chicken cubes
1½ cups (375 ml) water
1 cup uncooked rice
water
lemon juice
1 package frozen peas

1. Brown the pork and vegetables in some oil. Add the water in which at least 2 chicken cubes have been dissolved. Season to taste and simmer for at least 1 hour.
2. Add rice and sufficient liquid to twice cover the rice (about 1½ cups (375 ml). Cook again over low heat for about 1 hour. Just before serving add cooked frozen peas and the juice of 1 lemon.

Serves 4.

Pineapple Ham Loaf

1 lb (500 g) minced ham
1 lb (500 g) ground lean
  fresh pork
2 eggs
¾ cup soft breadcrumbs
¾ cup sour cream or milk
2 tablespoons tomato sauce
8 slices drained pineapple

Glaze:
1 cup brown sugar
½ cup (125 ml) pineapple
  syrup
2 tablespoons lemon juice
1 teaspoon prepared
  mustard

1. Mix all the ingredients together except the pineapple. Roll into a loaf and divide into 9 patties.
2. In a shallow ovenproof dish form a long roll placing the pineapple in between each pattie starting and finishing with meat.
3. Bake for 30 minutes in a slow oven 325°F (160°C). Take from oven and pour some of the mixture of brown sugar, pineapple syrup, lemon juice and mustard over the loaf and bake again for 1 hour basting every 20 minutes with the glaze.

Serves 8.

93

Pork Tenderloin with Cranberry Sauce

6 thick slices of pork tenderloin
chopped parsley
2 cloves garlic, crushed
salt and pepper
4 tablespoons (80 g) butter
1 tablespoon flour
milk

½ cup sour cream
4 tablespoons cranberry
    sauce
3 tablespoons brandy
3 apples cored, cooked and
    sliced

1. Make a hole through the middle of the slices and stuff with parsley, garlic and salt and pepper.
2. Heat 2 tablespoons of butter in a frying pan and toss the meat in the hot butter for a minute. Set aside.
3. Add the rest of the butter to the pan and stir in the flour and add enough milk so as to make the sauce smooth. Return the meat to the pan and cover and simmer for 30 minutes turning once or twice so as not to catch.
4. When the pieces are cooked add the sour cream, cranberry sauce and brandy. Check the seasoning and bring to the boil.
5. Serve on a large platter with apple rings on each piece of meat and the sauce poured over with a dot of cranberry sauce on top of each apple ring.

Serves 6.

Index

Mild beef curry 33
Mint jelly 22
Mint lamb chops 64
Mint sauce 17
Mixed meat rolls 59
Moussaka 77
Mushroom sauce 17

Orange lamb 73
Orange pork chops 86
Orange stuffing 22
Oriental lamb 65
Oxtail Plaka style 49

Pepper steak 23
Pineapple ham loaf 93
Plum sauce 19
Pork and apple pie 87
Pork chop roll 89
Pork chops (shoulder) 84
Pork chops with prunes 85
Pork Satay 89
Pork Swedish Style 81
Pork Tenderloin 90
Pork Tenderloin Italian Style 93
Pork Tenderloin with Cranberry sauce 94
Pork with honey 85
Pot roast with macaroni 38
Pressed beef tongue 48

Quick beef curry 33
Quick mint sauce 18

Rolled rib roast of beef with Yorkshire pudding 32
Rolled shoulder of veal with fruity rice stuffing 51
Roast beef with oyster stuffing 31
Roasted lamb shanks 76
Roast loin of pork with stuffed apples 82
Roast pork Oriental style 83
Roasted veal with mushrooms 50
Royal broil 28

Sausages Jambalaya 88
Sausage rolls 41
Savory chops 65
Savory ground beef 39
Schnitzel Traudy style 53
Sesame beef kebabs 28
Scotch eggs 36
Shaslik Russian style 68
Shepherds pork pie 87
Shish kebabs 67
Spanish pork chops 84
Spareribs of beef or pork 89
Spiced corned silverside with fruit glaze 47
Spicy lamb shanks 75
Spicy lamb shoulder chops 66
Steak Argentine 31

Steak with prunes 30
Stifado 30
Sweet and sour lamb 76
Swiss steak 27
Tomato and wine sauce 18
Tongue in breadcrumbs 47
Tripe Yugoslavia 48

Veal birds with raisins 57
Veal curry with brazil nuts 55
Veal escalopes with ham and cheese 53
Veal Goulash 56
Veal knuckle pie 57
Veal in vermouth 54
Veal roast 51
Veal rolls with wine 54
Veal with bacon and herb stuffing 52
Veal steak with pork filling 55

Wiener schnitzel 52
Wine marinade 19